HEAVENS' LEVELS

Walk with me
Truth remorse forgiveness hope

Author Sharon L Burke

Forward Sharon M Irizarry

Order this book online at www.trafford.com
or email orders@trafford.com

Most Trafford titles are also available at major online book retailers.

Printed in the United States of America.

ISBN: 978-1-4269-3645-6 (sc)

*Our mission is to efficiently provide the world's finest, most comprehensive book publishing
service, enabling every author to experience success. To find out how to publish your book,
your way, and have it available worldwide, visit us online at www.trafford.com*

Trafford rev. 7/28/2010

 www.trafford.com

North America & international
toll-free: 1 888 232 4444 (USA & Canada)
phone: 250 383 6864 ♦ fax: 812 355 4082

To my Daughter Jennifer,

Your faith, spirituality and your strength are what kept me going every
time I thought I could go no further.
Thank you for being who you are.
I Love You,
Mom

Epigraph

We prepare for the end of our life by making sure we have life insurance to take care of those we leave behind so they can pay the bills send our children on to college and cover the expense of our funeral costs. We make sure to leave a bit of ourselves in our children by teaching them values and giving them love. We are ready to close our eyes for that final sleep, but are you prepared for where you are going to be when you wake on the other side, where you will spend your eternity? Will peace and love pass with you or are you about to pay the price for every infraction you have ever committed while living here on earth?

FORWARD

I met Sharon Burke about 30 years ago. Her sister Pat and I were friends and she introduced us.

We became fast friends. We were both young mothers with small children and living with the daily struggles of being a parent.

Not long after our friendship began, Sharon had a dream, a dream that began to infiltrate her sleeping and waking hours. She would wake and be compelled to write down what she saw in her dream, soon visions started that had no rhyme or reason when they would appear. During the visions she would jot down notes or spend moments, sometimes hours on her word processor with no conception of time just the compulsion to keep writing what she saw.

Sometimes the visions frightened her because she would find pages of notes and scraps of paper that she had no recollection of writing. Sharon will tell you that she didn't write this from her own talents, but that she was guided by another invisible force, and yet she didn't ignore what was presented to her and compile boxes of text to organize into book form.

Years passed and she continued to write. Then tragedy struck. Her beautiful and talented daughter was diagnosed with incurable cancer. Jessica passed at the age of 14 years. Sharon was devastated but her faith wrapped its arms around her and she went on. Then her precious grand son, Jeremy died of SIDs. Two horrific events in her life and still she went on with a strength given to her from a far greater being. She continued to write. Her only son George died from an anuerysim shortly after Jeremy. How much suffering is one woman supposed to carry and keep her sanity? Yet she went on with a grace many wished they had. Her faith again cloaked her with serenity.

After these tragedies, Sharon s visions struck with a vengeance. She was writing more and faster than ever. She will tell you that the tragedies in her life prepared her for the job she was given to do.

She was a messenger who witnessed the eternity we are destined to serve if we don't change our ways and ask for forgiveness, a last chance for humanity to save itself from an eternity of sorrow.

Once the book was about to be finished she was guided by a silent force to make a C.D. Sharon said all the people who recorded for her were sent to her. Each a perfect match to the guide they were portraying. I was chosen and gladly participated. Feeling honored to be a part of such an awakening. Sadly, while we were recording the C.D. her beloved husband Dan had a massive heart attack and joined Jessica, Jeremy, and George in heaven.

When you read this book, you may find that it frightens you, or comforts you or answers many of your questions about our next life. It is not intended to frighten but to enlighten you and hopefully bring you peace.

Sharon doesn't know why she was chosen and some may think she just sat down and wrote a book. Knowing her as I do, I believe she was a chosen messenger and I have been blessed with her friendship and guidance.

Some people will laugh at the author and her visions. I do not doubt her and hope that when you read this book, you will understand that the rivers of thought that ran through the authors head and fingers were given her and are being passed on to you. She believes, as I and many others believe that she was given this gift to bring to humanity to save their souls and prepare for them a place in paradise.

Who better then Sharon to be chosen to bring this knowledge to mankind, she has suffered more than most of us and through her grief she has gained solace in her own personal belief, in Our Father and His son. Her strength has come from her suffering her book has come from her belief in God and as she was instructed, she is bringing this guide to you.

S. M. Irizarry

INTRODUCTION

Have you ever wondered where you would be after you die? For me it all began after a near fatal car accident when I woke up in heaven. There I was greeted by two angels Thomas and Issias. I was told that I did not die but that I was brought there as a messenger to bring all that I see back to earth with me in a last effort to save mankind. I walked through the most glorious gardens, with magnificent flowers and foliage trees that bore every kind of fruit known to man. Issias and I walked along a marble path along the water's edge until we reached a building made completely of marble, there I met some of the angles regarded as the guardians I attend conference in the arena where I am introduced as the messenger. After conference Zepherus and I begin our journey through the twenty levels of heaven. There I am witness to the most amazing and wonderful sights of heaven where God lives on the top of his mountain with his chosen ones. From there I travel through the most horrific and terrifying levels imaginable. I experience going from the most peace and love I had ever known to the purest evil where I am filled with fear and terror. I am warned many times on this journey that I must remember all that I see to bring back to earth with me so that mankind knows where and how his eternity will be spent. Man must prepare now while he still has a chance to make the right choices. My only hope is that I will bring back to earth with me as clear of a picture as I have seen although there were many times throughout this journey I had wished I could forget the things I saw.

Because of this walk I have been able to incorporate the greatest joys and sorrows of my life into this book. To those of you who believe and to those of you that do not, may God bless you and keep you safe.

THE AWAKENING

Sharon:

My mind was in a haze as I woke to the sound of beeps and pumps pounding in my head.

I tried to focus as I scanned the room.

What am I doing here, in a hospital?

As my head began to clear and I began to remember....

Oh my God...!!! Oh my God...!!!

Contents

CHAPTER ONE

The Beginning

The morning began just like any other morning. I woke to my husband Dan's voice calling me to get up as I stumble to the dining room I was greeted by our happy, huge, bouncy dog Motley. Tail wagging and heavy breathing was the first sign that told me he was anxiously waiting for me to take him to the back door and let him out. Well I neither jump nor do I run in the morning. This however is one concept he hasn't gotten yet, even though he is eight years old and lived under our domain since he was six weeks old.

My next greeting comes from Dan, my all cheerful, smiling, and perky in the morning husband Dan he still does not comprehend the fact that I do not speak, nor do I hear well in the morning because he cheerfully carries on a conversation to the bobbing of my head every morning.

After I've had my first cup of coffee, yawned and stretched a bit, spoke a few words, this seems to be some kind of acknowledgement to Motley that I am now alive and he can proceed to whine, cry and just about climb onto my lap to get my attention until I finally get up and let him out so he can, well, let's just say go out and play.

By this time I'm ready for my second cup of coffee. Dan by now is already dressed and ready to leave for work. Although I'm a little more aware of life around me I'm still not ready for the challenges of the day I take my time, throw on some jeans, a t-shirt, tie back my hair, splash cold water on my face and I'm ready to go. I let the dog in and try to remember what it was that I promised myself I wouldn't forget to do this morning. Oh well, it will come to me I reassure myself. I grabbed my jacket just as Dan called for me to hurry or we would be late and traffic would be heavy.

The drive to work was always beautiful. We made it a point to take the beach side drive to work every morning, rain or shine, because every sunrise was more spectacular that the day before. It was a though God took his hand and painted us a new picture every day.

As the sun rises over the ocean and breaks through the clouds the most brilliant colors take form. Orange, purple, pink and yellows shifting and dancing across the sky every passing minute until the sun in its glory stands alone. The ocean, magnificent and powerful with its silver spun waves creates a treasure in the sand as it sparkles like diamond as the waves meet the shore. Who could resist this splendor, all this peace? It's an image that lasts within your mind and soul all day long. You carry it in your heart and pass it on to those you meet.

As we approach our shop Dan begins to fumble for his keys, I have a key on my keychain that would open the door but he is out of the car and ready to open the door before I even have my seatbelt off. I watch Dan as he approaches the store and he still looks the same as he did twenty five years ago with his broad shoulders and strong arms, his blonde hair although a little thinning shows little sign of gray and his eyes are the color of the sky when the sun shines on his face. His features are quite handsome and gentle and after all these years he still brings peace to my soul and laughter to my heart, I love our little store, it's not much and it will never make us rich but we're happy here and when we open the door in the morning I love the smell of juicy fruit gum, the salty air and the lingering scent of jasmine from the night before. I look around and do a quick inventory of the things I'll have to pick-up on my morning rounds. Most of the items we sell such a t-shirts, novelty items, purses, trinkets and beach wear we have shipped to us. Other items such as candy, gum, paper products and coffee, I pick-up and bring back with me when I return later.

Well now that Dan is all settled in it's time for me to start my day. First shopping, then home to shower and change, put on some make-up, tidy my hair and back to the shop I go. Once I'm in the house I am greeted by Motley. After he does his ten laps around the kitchen table, through the parlor door and around the coffee table then back again he always gets his doggie cookies. I throw of my shoes, scold Motley for having been up on the couch, I pour myself another cup of coffee and call my daughter Jennifer on the phone. This ritual has not varied in the last eight years. I sometimes wonder how I became so steadfast in some of the things I do, but I guess it's probably, because I like order in my life I find it just makes life easier. We talk for a few minutes about the baby, Georgialynn, her husband Kenny, dad, the store, school, and whatever else comes to mind. This morning she reminded me that I had to make dinner reservations for tonight. At least once a month we make sure to have a night out for dinner. This month it's my turn to decide where we're going and I get to make the reservations. Ah! So that's what I wanted to remember to do this morning. I knew it would come to me. We say our goodbyes she is running late for work and has to take Georgialynn to daycare yet. I rinse out my cup, stick it in the dishwasher with the cups from this morning, gather up the flowers I bought this morning to take to the cemetery and out the door I go. I just wanted to say hello to my daughter Jessica, my son Georgie, and my grandson Jeremy. Although they are no longer here physically they're always with me spiritually. I think back to a time, years ago when life was so easy, to a time before the word cancer became an everyday part of our vocabulary. To a time when my Jessica was happy and healthy and her biggest problem was how late she could stay out. Then I remember the words ewing sarcoma. Ewing sarcoma what is that I remember thinking. Well after eight long months of chemo, radiation, surgery, tears and shock I knew all about Ewing sarcoma and how devastating it was. I watched as it took my beautiful daughter and drained every ounce of life out of her. I watched as it took her last breath of life from her. Ewing sarcoma, yes I knew exactly what a Ewing sarcoma was. It's been a long ten years and the pain has subsided and peace, love and faith have replaced most of the pain, most of my sorrow. I will miss her forever and the fourteen years we had together were not enough, but I know she is safe and protected in the arms of God. I know too, that I will see her again someday, to hold her and to see her beautiful smile.

It seems as though we had just begun to find some normalcy in our lives when our first grandchild was born three years later. I can't begin to express the joy he brought into our lives. Jennifer took the death of her sister harder than anyone. She not only lost a sister, she lost her best friend. From the day Jessica was brought from the hospital they bonded. Although they were only fifteen months apart Jennifer wanted to play mom. I made it a point not to call Jessica my baby or the baby but to address her as your baby sister and it worked. I let her hold her and lay beside her, help to change her and bathe her. Before I knew it they were inseparable and this is just how it was, they were the girls forever.

So, with the birth of her first child came a new love, a love more precious and tender than she had ever known before. She gave this baby every ounce of love she had in her heart. She laughed, she truly laughed again. He had replaced the pain and put it in its proper place. Jeremy gave her time to forget the pain, as he did with all of us. But this joy was to be short lived. Six weeks after Jeremy entered this world he was called back home. Sudden infant death syndrome, something else we knew nothing about. The only thing I knew is that it took this wonderful, precious baby away from us and threw us right back into a world of sorrow.

I thank God today for giving Jeremy to Jennifer, even though it was for only a little while, because no one could have loved him more. Her tenderness, love and joy are what she shared with this child and this is what he took back to heaven with him.

I did not know how we would make it through this. How could we survive? How would Jennifer ever be able to come to terms with such a great loss, he was her world. I by the grace of God have little memory of that day. Most of what I witnessed is buried deep within my mind. Those memories I do remember I wish I could change. The look of terror as Jennifer ran into my room screaming for me to help her, that Jeremy was not breathing, I thought I was having a nightmare as I jumped out of bed, but when I saw the doll like look in his eyes and on his face I knew this was not a dream. I had seen this look on Jessica's face the night she died. I screamed for Dan to help us. As he grabbed for Jeremy he began to perform mouth to mouth resuscitation on him. I ran to the phone to call 911. I know I must have sounded hysterical as I screamed at the operator to help. I thought that I sounded perfectly clear as I gave her the details but she kept telling me to put someone on the phone that was coherent. How many ways can you say, send an ambulance, my grandson is not breathing I yelled at her. Dan grabbed the phone and thanked the operator. They're on their way he said gently, still holding the baby in his arms. I could see Jennifer from the corner of my eye as I ran to the front porch. "He's o.k. mom", I heard her say, "he just opened his eyes, and I think he's breathing. She was rubbing his back with one hand and holding his hand with her other. I saw Dan wipe what looked like a drop of blood from his little nose. The fire truck was coming up the street it seemed to take them forever. I remember going out to the porch and I was yelling for them to hurry. I remember them coming into the house. I remember them standing in front of me. I remember seeing my sister and my nephew running from next door and I can hear myself screaming for my nephew to help us. I know I must have terrified him.

When my neighbor from across the street came over to stay with me I told her to leave. She told me Dan had asked her to stay with me. He didn't want me to be alone. I said I was not alone, that they were in the kitchen that no one had left. Still to this day I do not remember anyone leaving. I don't remember the firemen walking past me with the baby in his arms, nor do I remember Dan, Jennifer or my nephew Jamie leaving the house. They tell me they tried to get me to go to the hospital with them. After my neighbor left I went into the kitchen to see how Jennifer was and they were all gone. I thought they went out the back door. Where did they go, I thought? I ran to the front door to see if I could find them, but the only ones I saw were my sister and a friend from down the street. I asked them where they were going and they said they were going to the hospital. I must have lost my mind, I flipped, and I began screaming at them to go home there was no reason for them to go to the hospital everything was fine. They looked at me as though I was nuts. My sister got into the car and drove away.

I then phoned my older sister Pat and asked her to come over, that I was scared. I told her I thought Jeremy had died, but I did not know where anyone was because they wouldn't tell me anything. Needless to say they were at my door within minutes. They had called another neighbor from down the street and were told the baby was taken out of the house by a fireman and that he looked limp and lifeless as they put him in the ambulance. Jennifer and Dan went in the ambulance to the hospital Jamie drove behind in his car.

I went to the front door to see if anyone was coming and I saw our friends and neighbors standing on their porches and in the street crying. Oh God, I thought, its true Jeremy is gone.

My son Georgie had been out of town, he flew home that afternoon to be with his sister. There he stayed, by her side every minute. He felt every depth of her pain. The death of her son nearly destroyed my daughter. But somehow she found the strength to survive. Her relationship with her brother grew stronger as he got older. Things like music, clothes and friends soon made them the best of friends and they could talk, truly talk, after all they knew each other's pain. They knew each other's history. Who else would know your most precious secrets they could laugh or cry together? They understood one another.

Soon after Jeremy s death Georgie met Liane and they fell in love. They were so young, but love, I guess, does not see age as a deterrent. You could see the love they felt for one another. It was as though no one else existed when they were together. I worried that they would not be responsible and lectured them both about sex and pregnancy, but a lot of good that did. A few months later they were going to be parents. They were a little nervous, but accepting of the situation. It was their last year in high school and they both decided to stay in school and get their diploma and they did. So along came Jenica, happy, healthy and the apple of everyone's eye. Liane stayed with her parents and went on to college. Georgie stayed at home and also went to school, found a part-time job that led to full time work, but it was hard for him. He decided to quit school and keep working, after all the baby needed things and he could go back to school later. Well three months after Jenica was born they told me that Liane was pregnant again. This time I don't think they were ready to be parents again but they made it through all the mixed emotions and after all they were still very much in love. So along came Christian, a little twin of his dad. The kids were a handful for them but they handled it well. Just before Georgie's twentieth birthday he decided to move out of our house and get his own apartment. He felt like he needed time to himself. "After all, I am a man now" he said. Well he wasn't a man to me yet, but Georgie always did what he thought was right for himself anyway. Jennifer helped him set up his apartment and they spent a lot of time together, they were truly friends. But that was soon to come to an end.

On one hot summer night in June, my son was found dead on his living room floor. He was only nineteen years old. A brain aneurysm what a what, I thought. Once again we were thrown into a whirlwind of emotions. How could we ever deal with another loss? How will we ever survive? I decided to leave work early and stop to see Georgie on my way home. His apartment was only a short block from my house and I was concerned because he had been having some really bad headaches and I wanted to see whether or not he had gone to the doctors. He had promised me when I talked to him the night before that if they weren't any better he would see a doctor in the morning. When I turned onto his street I saw a group of his friends standing around the house. I then noticed Liane sitting on the porch her face buried in her hands. She looked as though she was crying. I jumped out of my car and as I looked at the faces on the people standing there and I knew something was terribly wrong. Liane's mother was running down the street, that's when I noticed the police car. I then heard someone say "I'm not telling her." "Telling me what?" I thought. Then this crushing fear came over me, "Oh no", I thought "do not tell me Georgie is dead do not, please do not tell me this". I ran up the stairs to his apartment but the police would not let me in as I begged for them to let me see my son. Jennifer came running down the stair. "Oh my God mom, he's dead. Georgie's dead." "I have to go home now ", I heard myself say and I turned and walked away. The police began to ask me some questions but I could not answer them. I could not watch another one of my children be brought out dead before my eyes.

I began to head to my car but I heard Jennifer yell for me not to get into the car and she grabbed the keys out of my hand. I don't know where she went but then I heard my sister call to me as she ran up to me from behind. She was crying and telling me she was so sorry, than she followed me home. The only words I could hear myself saying were no, no, no." As I walked into my house I was trembling. "Dan", I thought. I have to talk to Dan Oh my God, how do I tell him? I picked up the phone to dial the number but I could not remember, I tried again but my mind would not work. I looked around for my purse. I know I have it written down somewhere. But my purse was gone I had somehow lost my purse between Georgie's house and home. When I started crying hysterically because I couldn't find my purse, Kathy promised to go and find it for me. As I waited for my sister to return the phone rang and it was Dan. " What's going on with George? Donnie called and said the police were at his apartment." Dan asked. "Dan, listen to me, George is gone I don't know what happened but he was found dead in his apartment. Dan didn't realize what was being said he just asked me to come and pick him up that he was closing the store. Just then Jennifer came in with her boyfriend Kenny and he said he would pick Dan up for me. Within what seemed like only minutes he was back home with Dan. "He should have stayed with us he would still be o.k. if he had stayed with us." Dan said as he turned and walked into Georgie's room and shut the door. I let him be. I knew he wanted to be alone with his thoughts, alone with his memories. When he came out of the room a little while later he seemed to have aged ten years but he would not sit still long enough to listen as the details were being discussed. He either got up and left the room or tried to change the subject. My uncle Matt and his wife Connie made all the funeral arrangements. Dan made one excuse after another so he wouldn't have to go. I knew this was a shock to him, but I also could see that he wasn't dealing with the loss. It seemed as though, if he could stay at a distance, he wouldn't have to believe Georgie was gone.

He actually got up the next morning and went to work. He didn't wake me, though. He phoned Jennifer to tell her to have me call him if I needed him for anything. It seemed as though I just floated through the next few days. We had one visit after another. Georgie's' friends were all wonderful. They promised to never forget Georgie, and to stop by and visit often. A promise most of them kept.

It took time, once again, to put our lives back together. Dan went on to working twelve hours a day, six days a week. I on the other hand started working part time, four hours a day, three days a week. Dan and I learned to grieve in our own separate way. We accepted each other's privacy. After all, grieving was a very personal thing. We talk about the child in a positive way, always remembering the life, not lingering on the death. This way it keeps that child alive in our memory forever. I could not miss these children any more than I do, but even through all the pain, I sometimes find solace on knowing they are safe in God's hands. No one could ever hurt them. They are out of harm's way.

Jennifer was so angry. I think anger was her way of coping with this newest tragedy. And who more could she be angry with, then God almighty. Why would God take all those that were most precious to her? But her anger was put to rest by God himself. He would not allow her to be angry with Him. Her anger caused her to begin her search for the truth. Where were Jessica, Jeremy and Georgie? What did God do with them? So her search began. Exactly what was Gods promise to us and where else would you begin, then the Bible itself. God's own words to us, his children, and the bottom line was life after death. Paradise, a place where there is no pain a place without sorrow. Somewhere that hate and crime do not exist. Heaven, a place so full of love and peace, that doing what God asks us to here on earth, would be the only choice we would make. She began to understand that the people she loved so much and lost were not lost forever. They were only in a different place. It was as though they had moved away from home and we would see them again. They were by no means, gone forever.

I myself found my connection with God after the birth of my first child. Prior to that time I did not understand. I did not truly believe there was a God. Although I had been raised a Christian, and went to a catholic school, I still didn't have a clue as to who God really was or what his words meant to us. But this miracle of life I witnessed when my daughter was born began to raise questions in my mind. It wasn't the physical aspect, but the emotional aspect of having this child that made me begin my search. This kind of love was so deep, so unique it had to come from the soul itself.

As I looked back on my life, I saw that God had always been with me on my journey as I searched for my own answers pertaining to God and our purpose here on earth. I then discovered that God had provided me with many gifts in my life. There were many times that I was aware of things to come before they happened, and I never questioned where it came from. I called it premonition. My grandmother called it a gift, an inheritance from her because she had it all her life, too. She knew, she just knew things that had happened or things that were about to happen. You could never tell a lie to grandma and get away with it. She would tell you step by step exactly what did happen, and we as children thought all grown -ups could do that.

Jennifer also has grandmas gift, a gift she is just beginning to understand and develop. When we talked about it for the first time, she told me she was always afraid as a child, because none of her friends could do what she could do. Sometimes they got mad at her when her predictions came true. "It's just, knowing sometimes, about what's going to happen. Other times I can actually see things happen, like seeing a movie in my mind. I think I'm wacked, but when they happen I sometimes get a little scared. Other times I'm really excited", she explained.

My personal experience with the gift has only showed me that this is not something you can bring about yourself. It just happens. You might be talking to a friend and all of a sudden you just know their child is sick or that their husband is cheating on them. You find yourself pushing back visions in your mind because you feel like you're intruding in their privacy. In a week, when they are telling you what happened to them, you bite your tongue so you don't say, "Yea, I already knew that". A feeling may come over you that this person is in danger or that something good is going to happen to them. What do you do? Do you tell them to be careful, do you tell them to take a new job or buy a lottery ticket? No you keep it to yourself. There are exceptions, though. One time when I was sitting in a fast food restaurant with Jennifer and Jessica, when they were little, four men walked in and sat down in about across from us. I had this over powering feeling of danger for them. I tried to push it back but I couldn't. I kept seeing this blue pickup truck on the 190 expressway being hit by a tractor trailer and although I couldn't see their faces clearly I knew it was them trapped inside. As hard as I tried to walk past them without saying anything I couldn't help myself I just had to stop and ask them if they were taking the 190 home. They looked at me as if I wanted something as though I was going to ask them for a ride somewhere. I heard someone say "No we're not ", and I smiled out of embarrassment and turned to walk away. " Why do you want to know if we were taking the expressway?" another man asked me and I reluctantly told them what I had seen. The man that had just told that they were not talking the 190 spoke up and said" We were going to take the express way home but we won't taking it now." They knew they just knew that what I had told them would save their lives.

At times this gift from God also terrified me. Jessica was a very unique child, she was bright, smart and easy, from the beginning she was easy with the world around her. She never got overly excited about any situation she just took things in stride. I was amazed at the way her mind worked even as a little child I would tell my family and friends to listen to her talk listen to the way she thinks. No matter what would happen, she always remained calm and logical she could always make me laugh. A shining star at three, she won first place in an art show. The following year she graduated pre-kindergarten and read us her diploma. At five she was reading at a second grade level and took part in an educational commercial promoting the early childhood program for school. All this before she was in first grade. And this continued throughout grammar school, winning awards in athletics, music, and poetry she was inducted in to the junior honor society for her academic standing in the eighth grade. This child was loved by everyone, family, friends, peers and teachers. She had a true understanding of what made people tick and she had a knack of making everyone she came in contact with feel comfortable. She was one of Gods shinning stars. But all of this, created a fear within me, I wondered, was God giving her all of this so young because he was going to take her away from me? Yes, and he did take her home with him.

I also had these same feelings with my son George he was the youngest of my three children. Georgie was daring and independent and after the death of his sister and nephew he became reckless taking chances that I considered dangerous. But he would not listen as I tried to express my concerns he was after all a young boy and young boys do believe they are invincible. He always told me not to worry whenever I expressed my fears "I will be fine ", was his favorite line to me. I somehow knew I would lose him too.

A gift, a premonition or an insight no matter what you call it I once again knew. It somehow became perfectly clear to me that your days are numbered from the day you are born. You may live a life time escaping death only because death was not ready for you. It does not matter if you are a six week old infant, a fourteen year old child or a sixty year old man. If you live your life on the edge or live like a saint it just doesn't matter as to when your time is at hand to leave this earth.

The trip to the cemetery always sends my head swimming, it's always one flash back after another. I sit and talk for a while and then I say my good-bys. My heart aches from the loneliness I feel I wish I could see them now, I wish I could tell them how much they are missed and how much I love them. I wipe the tears from my eyes, take a deep breath and walk away. I promise that I will soon return as I climb in to my car and drive away. I remember thinking "what is that truck doing?", as it slid through the intersection. The sound of screeching breaks, metal against metal and something warm on my neck. I grabbed my neck to see what was causing me so much pain. "I'm bleeding to death" I thought as I felt a sharp object lodged in my neck. Daylight began to fade around me and the sound of sirens became faint in the distance "no, do not fall asleep" I told myself but I could not stop myself from drifting away.

I watched from above the room as the doctors and nurses performed emergency surgery on me. I listened as they chatted nonchalantly "This doesn't look promising" I heard the doctor say as he removed his gloves and left the operating room.

"Now we wait, the next twenty four hours will be the most critical". He said as he spoke to Dan and Jennifer. They were terrified as they listened for any shred of hope from the doctor "Go home and get some sleep, she is resting quietly for now and you will need your rest, the both of you go home"! He repeated as he patted them on their backs as they walked down the hall.

I suddenly felt as though I was being guided through some sort of wind tunnel. I was terrified as I was being pulled further and further away. I could see and I could hear but I did not feel any pain. I remember thinking, "Am I dead"?"No I can't be I can't do this to Jennifer and Dan, I have to go back" But I continued going forward through space and time. I could see my life go by as though it were bring rewound on a video. I began to see a ray of light ahead of me and now for some reason I had no fears for Dan or Jennifer as I had before somehow I knew they would be alright, I knew I would see them again."

CHAPTER TWO

The Arrival

As I passed through the light I lost all consciousness. I woke on a highly polished hard wood table it had four posts, each post had carvings of angels. The table was surrounded by people they were all wearing yellow robes. I was directed to go into a room directly across from the table and change. I wanted to ask questions but I could not get them out. As I stepped down from the table I looked to the left of me and then to the right and for as far as I could see there were people just like myself they had the same look of confusion on their faces . Across from their tables I also saw doors. As directed I went through the door and entered a room that looked just like a changing room it had a full length mirror and a bench to sit on, hanging on a hook, was a tan robe for me to change into. I could not believe what I saw in the mirror I was covered in blood, I had a six inch gash in my neck and the side of my face was bruised and swollen. As I touched my face and neck I was amazed to find that I had no pain and as I began to undress I watched in amazement as my body began to heal itself right before my eyes. The bruising, gash and swelling all began to reverse themselves I watched as the wrinkles from my face faded and all of my old scars vanished. I stood there looking at a perfect me. I still looked my age but without any of the imperfections. I slipped on the robe and turned to open the door only to find there was no handle on it. I pushed on the wall to the right of me and then to the left of me but nothing happened as I turned and pushed the wall behind me it began to move. As I opened the door I saw the most incredible light that I had ever seen. It was the warmth of the sun seen through my eyes. As I stepped through the door I saw groups of people standing around talking and laughing with each other, each one smiled and nodded their greeting to me as they looked my way.

Woman:

"There is no one here to greet you."

Sharon:

"I heard this voice behind me say. As I turned to see who was talking to me, there was a woman reaching out to touch my hand."

Woman:

"We are here to greet those who pass over and reunite them with their loved ones. You must be here to meet with Thomas and Issias. They will be here in a moment, peace be with you my child."

Sharon:

"Thomas, who is Thomas I thought". The woman smiled softly, turned and walked away. I watched her as she held her arms open to a man that came through the entrance, she hugged him and spoke to him as she led him to another man standing at the edge of a path, there she kissed him on his cheek and they went their separate ways. I had this overwhelming feeling of peace and love that penetrated my body.

I had no fears or worries, I felt no pain or sorrow there was no self consciousness, inadequacies or confidence. I no longer felt the need to judge, nor did I have a sense of being judged myself. I felt none of the human frailties that touched mankind. Peace, love and joy filled my heart. I knew without a doubt that I had entered the threshold of heaven. I remember thinking heaven really is the clouds as I looked around me. I felt as though I was walking in the sky itself as soft blue and white surrounded me as far as I could see. Suddenly out of nowhere two men wearing turquoise robes approached me.

Thomas:

"I am Thomas, and this is Issias, we bring you greetings of great joy."

Issias:

'Welcome, child."

Sharon:

"Issias extended his hand to me in friendship. When I touched his hand it had a calm almost serene touch to it, like that of a mother touching her child. As I looked into his eyes they spoke the words trust me, and

I did. From that very first moment I knew no harm would come to me here."

Thomas:

"You are wondering why you are here."

Sharon:

"Thomas spoke gently as though he wanted to reassure me that no harm would come to me. "I thought I had died and this was heaven" I told him."

Thomas:

"Well some of what you say is true, this is heaven but you have not died. You were brought here as a messenger to bring the truth back to earth."

Sharon:

"I did not quite understand what Thomas was saying to me, I heard his words but I was totally baffled."

Thomas:

"Issias will take you on your journey to the transition room. There you will wait for Samarious, he will introduce you to Mary and she will explain all you need to know. I will see you again before your journey home, have no fears".

Sharon:

"Thomas kissed my cheek in a farewell greeting, nodded his head to Issias and walked away."

Issias:

"I know you have many questions, just be patient for a little while and they will be answered. You will leave knowing much more then you could ever imagine. This is a very important gift that you have been given, and a very difficult task lies ahead of you."

Sharon:

"Issias seemed much at ease as he spoke to me, I was curious but I too was at ease. I was in awe at the beauty that surrounded me. We walked through a meadow of emerald green grass with pearly white dew. There were flowers of every kind imaginable, and their brilliance was as pure as a rainbow when seen through a prism. The roads were made of marble and felt cool to the feet as you walked.

As we walked we approached a foot bridge that crossed over a stream the water was crystal clear, and the sand in the stream was pure and coral in color. There were magnificent fish with hews of aqua, and oranges, bright greens, deep reds, golden yellows, glittering silver and lavender. I have never seen anything that brought so much joy to my heart. The bridge was also made of marble."

Issias:

"If you look closely at the hand rails you will see a map carved into them, there are pathways and gardens, waterfalls and mountains, forests, jungles, deserts and buildings. If you look just ahead you can see the transition house."

Sharon:

"Issias pointed to a building to the right of me that sat on the water edge. Buildings in heaven I thought. "This is not at all what I had expected heaven to be like." The building was also made of marble, but as we approached it I noticed that the doorway and windows were something entirely unknown to me, on the lawn in front of the building stood the statue of an angle. It looked exactly like the angles painted by Michael Angelo. The features were perfect, strong yet gentile, its wings swept down and touched the ground, and it held a child in its arms. As we walked, Issias told me what to expect once we entered the transition area."

Issias:

"You will meet with Samarious in the transition section there you will meet with some of the angels that have just returned from earth. These angles would be the one they call guardians. The guardians return with their charge once their charge passes on. The guardians have spent the life time of their charge on earth with them. They have protected them and tried to guide them to do what was right and they are the ones that guide them through the tunnel on their return to heaven. The transition area is a greeting area and a place for the guardians to catch up on all the news they missed while on earth."

Sharon:

"We came to the entrance of the building but instead of having to open the doors we just walked right through them."

Issias:

"I see this is something unusual to you. It is air that runs through the frame of the building and at each opening such as a window or doorway, the air seals the room, you can see through it and you can talk through it, you can also hear through it if you wish, unless you want privacy then with a voice command the air in turns into wispy clouds to prevent sound or visibility from coming through. We are here at the reception area you may wait for me here. I will return soon."

Sharon:

"The inside of the reception area was amazing I cannot describe the perfection, the organization and the co-operation, that existed there. Everyone, smiled, talked, worked and enjoyed what work they were doing. I began to understand how everything was connected. Everyone worked in harmony and joy. Laughter filled the air. Because of their love for the father, work was made joyous. They did not need material things for themselves life was simple, they wanted nothing because they needed nothing more then what God had provided for them. Issias's words brought me back from my thoughts."

Issias:

"It is wonderful here is it not."

Sharon:

"It is incredible I will never be able to find the words to describe what I have seen here."

Issias:

"You will see all, you will hear all and you will understand most. It will fill your heart and your mind the way of the words will come to you. Let us begin your journey from the beginning, here in the transition room. Watch and listen to as much as possible. See with your eyes, absorb with your heart. I shall return after my meeting with the holy mother, she will then send for you after the conference."

Sharon:

"Conference, I thought, what conference.

As I stood at the entrance to the transition room an angel approached."

Issias:

"Greetings Samarious, it is good to see you again my friend, this is the observer she is called Sharon, she will remain here with you until my return."

Sharon:

"Issias placed my hand on Samarious."

Issias:

"Go with him in peace."

Sharon:

Issias turned and walked away and Samarious led me through the entrance doors.

Entering the transition room was like entering a garden. There were over grown tree and plants, a water pool and flowers, if you could imagine every flower you have ever seen this is what exists in heaven. Marble tables and benches were scattered around. This was by no way any room I had ever set my eyes on before. Except for the fact that there were entrance areas I would have thought I was at an exotic resort on an island in the Bahamas."

Samarious:

"This is a wonderful place, and these are only a few of the gifts we receive from our father for our loyalty and obedience."

Sharon:

"There was much activity going on around me. Samarious was friendly and cheerful as he sat with me.

I turned around to admire the view when music began to play. Angels in blue robes began to bring huge bowls of fruit and set them on the tables. Bananas, oranges, peaches, guava, papaya, melons, grapes, pears, pineapples filled these wooden bowls, even the bowls of fruit were made to look beautiful. In between the pieces of fruit fresh cut flowers were placed. They even color coordinate in heaven. " I never thought you would need food in heaven, I just thought there would be no need for food here." I said to Samarious in an almost questioning way."

Samarious:

"You are correct in your thoughts. Food is not a need here, it is a pleasure. There is nothing to need for here it is all supplied to us by the father. We have always been with the father, before earth was created, before the stars in your universe began to shine or the oceans held life. We are Gods first creation. But we do not multiply and bring forth children we were created in his image we to are without the imperfections mankind has brought on to himself. We are called beta. You were created and given paradise on earth you were given free will to do what is right or to do what is not right. We have no free will we do not know how to do wrong and we do not understand the need to not do what the father has asked of us. When Lucifer was cast out of heaven because of his betrayal to the father, he was sent to earth. There he and his band of evil doers were to wander forever. When God created man and gave him earth and free will he soon realized Lucifer's strength. Because of Adam and Eve's betrayal he decided to send to earth guardians. To help protect man from Lucifer and his devils but Lucifer was strong and he could often convince man to do what is wrong. It is often easier to do what is wrong rather then what is right and this is how Lucifer gained his control over humans. He offers man pleasures, through drugs, spirits, control, sex, murder any crime committed by man is committed for self pleasure. Here we love our father, and we do not hesitate to do what is right to please him. We would not want it any differently. Lucifer remembers this and tries to offer these evils to man so that he can take them away from the father. He wants to hurt God by taking his children from him by taking their souls.

The guardians on the other side have the task of trying to direct man in the right direction. To do good which most times is the hardest choice to make. Sometimes our whispers cannot be heard over the voice of Satan, other times they are ignored, and then there are times they just don't care. When doing evil is so self satisfying and pleasing for him, and in return they are given many things, money above all is truly the route to an eternity in hell. Money itself is not evil the means of getting the money is what causes man to become evil. To harm innocent people to kill or to destroy another, to take what does not belong to you only to have greater things. Power has also become the ruin of man it has taken on a life of its own with the destruction it has caused to mankind. Now Satan has the control over free will and the sinner no longer wants to live in the light, he must live in the shadows, hide within his lies, alone in the darkness, tangled in his, own web of deceit. His mind can never rest never see beautiful thoughts because it is caught up in trying to connive, manipulate and control every situation to protect his true identity from those he encounters. The innocent must listen to their guardian, open up their hearts and mind and truly listen to the whispers. Satan cannot go where he is not welcome and with the help of your guardian you will be protected from the temptation to do evil."

Sharon:

"I hope that I can explain the wonder and beauty enough for them to want to change."

Samarious:

"I am afraid people will not change because of how beautiful it is here. You have much beauty on earth and they destroy it every day with their chemicals, bombs, fires, oil spills, clearing of the trees in the rain forests and the destruction of the ozone. This they do without hesitation. No, it will take much more for the humans to change then beauty. All this you will soon see and understand. Soon you will meet some of the guardians upon their arrival from earth. Their first stop will be the grading area this is where they leave their charges so they can be evaluated. The guardians give their evaluations to the graders they review it and grade your life on earth. After their evaluation they decide what the appropriate level is and where they will spend eternity."

Sharon:

"Samarious paused for a moment."

Samarious:

"I am very pleased to be the one chosen to help you on your journey. There have always been problems on earth but it has never been as violent and as destructive as it is now. We pray a messenger will help to change this and make people aware of what awaits them here."

Sharon:

"Issias then entered the room and explained to us that I would meet with Mary after conference, which will be held at the third ringing of the bells."

Issias:

"You will stay with Samarious until conference then you will go with Zephrus to your meeting with Mary. I too will be with you at this meeting. Some of what you need to know will be discussed at conference. Samariuos I will speak with you again at conference, until then peace be with you."

Samarious:

"Soon conference will begin and you will understand the order here. Because we love the father order is possible here. If more humans knew of the Father, and what lies ahead for them in eternity, it could bring more peace to those on earth."

Sharon:

"Samarious was then greeted by some of his friends. Now this I recognized as an angel for she had long flowing wings."

Jacodia:

"Samarious my dear friend it has been a very long time since we spoke last it is good to see you again. My journey was long this time."

Samarious:

"Jacodia my friend and Ar-kar-ea it brings such pleasure to see you both again, you have truly been missed since you left for your journey."

Sharon:

"Samarious was joyful as he speaks to his friends again."

Jacodia:

"We have arrived at a perfect time I understand there is to be a conference very soon, there is so much to hear about since our departure. Have you seen Tassari yet she came through the tunnel the same time as I did?"

Samarious:

"No I have not seen her yet, I am sure she will follow soon."

Sharon:

"Samarious looked around the room for a moment."

Samarious:

"I do see many faces that I have not seen in a long time though Jacodia."

Jacodia:

"There is news as to a messenger being sent to earth, I am grateful to hear this. There are so many things that are truly wrong there. It is as though our presence isn't even important to so many humans. They are on their way to the destruction of all mankind."

Samarious:

"Jacodia, I would like to introduce you to the observer. She is the one to carry the truth back to man.

She will be our messenger, our last act of hope."

Jacodia:

"May your journey home always find you safe and in peace with the lords blessing. You are truly blessed."

Sharon:

"Jacodia held my hand as she bent over and kissed my cheek."

Jacodia:

"Earth finds herself in much difficulty it saddens my heart to watch the destruction. People are so concerned with their own success and making money they don't think about the consequences of their deeds. The afterlife to them is not thought of as an extension of their life in eternity, it is only thought of as an end. They prepare for their burial and their financial support of those they leave behind but they are not prepared for the price they will have to pay once they take their final sleep and cross over the threshold into heaven.

I was fortunate during my stay David my charge was a good boy that grew to be a good man. He worked hard, had a lovely wife and taught his children well, their life was not always easy but their faith always got them through the hard times. David loved his wife his children and his lord. What more could you ask for in a charge he was open to my words and he feared the ways of Satan. His strength and integrity were always foremost. He will be greatly missed by his family and friends".

Samarious:

"You as a guardian were most fortunate indeed Jacodia there are so many charges that pay no attention to their guardians".

Sharon:

"Isn't it had for a guardian to see their charge make the wrong choice and ignore their advice?

Samarious looked at me as though he was searching for the right words to answer my question."

Samarious:

"The guardians do not judge what mankind does, they only try to direct and protect them from harm they are not capable of becoming emotionally involved nor do they interfere with the choices that their charge makes. They try to guide them in the right direction but the final choice is always of their own doing. It does not matter to the guardian what choice the charge makes if he does wrong he is the one that must pay the penalty for his disobedience to the father. There are charges that are well aware of guardians presence they have a special gift. These charges know without a doubt that they are being guided they talk to their guide and form a relationship to them. This type of charge can form a concern for the guardian and the guardian will follow that charge through grading and to his level. He will stay with him until he is comfortable and understands what has happened and where he is".

Sharon:

"At that moment Tasari entered the room."

Samarious:

"Tasari my dear friend it is wonderful to see you again I had thought you would have been here already when the others had arrived. Jacodia had asked about when she arrived a little while ago".

Tasari:

"I would have been here earlier but my charge was a six year old child and she was so worried about her parents being sad she had a hard time passing through. I didn't want to lose her if she decided to turn around and go back so I got permission to let her go back for a little while to see her mom and dad once she has settled in. It did help that her grandmother had passed recently though we brought her in to see her grandmother and it did help her tremendously. The child remembered the grandmother coming to play with her after her passing. It brought her much comfort".

Sharon:

"Tasari was beaming as she spoke of her charge."

Samarious:

"This is the exception to the rule."

Sharon:

Samarious laughed as he patted Tasari on her shoulder.

Samarious:

"We were just discussing the relationship between guardian and charge when you entered the room. I was explaining to the observer that guardians do not get emotionally involved with their charges and then you walked in only to prove differently. But this is a good thing it shows that there are exceptions even in heaven."

Sharon:

"At that moment the bells began to ring and every one began to leave to go to conference area. I saw Issias as he entered the room."

Issias:

"Samarious, I find everything is well."

Samarious:

"Yes Issias, it has been good the observer has listened and learned much about our ways at transition. She is ready to join us at the conference."

Sharon:

Issias held out his hand as a gesture of friendship and Samarious returned his greeting. "Issias then turned to me and put his arm around my shoulder. Issias said his good-bys for a moment."

Issias:

"I must leave you for now but I will see you again after your return from the levels with Zepherus, Samarious will be with you through conference. May the lord's love be with you throughout your journey."

Sharon:

"Issias nodded to Samarious turned and walked away."

Samarious:

"You will hear much at conference, listen closely and carry it with you to the levels you are to journey through. I know there are many questions you need answered, when you are at the meeting with Mary after the conference is over you may ask anything you need to know and she will tell you the best she knows how. I will stay with you for only a little longer. After the conference you and Zepherus will meet with Mary, than you will begin your decent through the levels of heaven. Zepherus will guide you safely, trust all he says and listen to what he tells you to do. Watch and remember everything you see. You must carry the heart of a beta with you."

Sharon:

"The bells rang a final time and Samarious led me through the arch into the arena."

Chapter Three

The Arena

Sharon:

"As we entered the arena we were approached by an angel wearing a tan robe and he wore a brown sash around one of his shoulders and a tan rope for a belt. Samarious: "Greetings Zepherus my friend this is Sharon the observer. She is the one you will take through the levels with you".

Zepherus:

"I have been looking forward to meeting with you since I heard that I would be the one to take you on your journey. There is much to see and much to carry back with you each step you take in heaven will help to prepare you for your journey home. I must take my leave and I now bid you farewell Sharon until we meet again after conference Samarious I will see you again after our return from the levels."

Samarious:

"Peace is with you Zepherus may your journey find you safe".

Sharon:

"Samarious and I followed a path that was off to the right of the main section of the arena. The main section was approximately the size of a football stadium. To the left there were levels of seats carved out of stone they were arranged in a half circle the width of the arena. The first level contained a seat with a desk top to the right of each seat and a viewing screen. The next level contained a seat with the desk top to the left and a viewing screen. This arrangement prevented anyone from blocking the view of the person behind them. At each level the seats were rotated. Directly in front of the seats there was a large table that also had viewers on it. Next to the viewers were folders and a microphone. Chairs were set up directly in front of each viewer. Behind the main table two smaller tables were set up the exact same way one to the right and one to the left. These tables did not have chairs though.

As I looked around the arena it was as though time had been turned back five thousand years. It was really beautiful almost jungle like with overgrown trees lush green plants and an array of huge colorful flowers. A waterfall could be seen through the trees and the air was fresh with the scent of jasmine. God truly knew how to create paradise. Samarious was so relaxed he smiled and took time to point out the birds and animals as they wandered throughout the jungle. I could actually see the love he carried inside of him his aura was the brightest I had ever seen. I wished that I could carry this feeling of unconditional love with me no matter where I went."

Samarious:

"If you look around you will see that the betas entering the arena are all wearing different color robes. Each color represents a duty they perform this way any one job could be identified just by seeing the color of robe they are wearing".

Sharon:

"There was much excitement as the betas entered the arena. Each one was handed an agenda as they entered the folios were the same color as the robe they wore.

The bells rang again and a woman entered and walked to the long table in the center of the arena. She wore her hair long and pulled back her eyes were crystal clear and her face glowed she was so beautiful she had the look of a new mother seeing her child for the first time. She wore a white cotton robe with a chiffon sash over the top of it the sash was trimmed in silver and it was tied with a silver belt. There were a few more betas that entered the arena behind her. They all smiled and grasped each others' hand in greeting. I remember thinking "Why can't the human race be like this toward each other, filled with peace and love". But then again we do not live in heaven."

Mary:

"Greetings my friends and welcome to conference. We have many issues that will be attended to but before we begin I would like to introduce a plan that in now in effect, I am sure most of you are already aware that we have chosen a messenger from earth to bring the Fathers words "Thy will be done on earth as it is in heaven "back to earth with her. The time is now to send our message to earth. It is our belief that a messenger is our last hope for mankind I'm not even sure that even with a glimpse into heaven they will change but at least we will have tried to give them a chance at eternal happiness. Our messengers name is Sharon she is seated with Samarious".

Sharon:

"With that Mary held out her arm and directed it to Samarious and myself. Everyone rose and applauded as they looked our way."

Mary:

"My name is Mary and it is with an open heart that I welcome you".

Sharon:

"Mary walked from behind the table to where Samarious and I were seated and she put her arms around me and whispered to me."

Mary:

"Remember child what you see and hear at conference will help to carry you on your journey and it will be up to you to present what you see and hear to those on earth. We will talk again before you go to the levels."

Sharon:

"Mary then turned and walked back to her table. She waved her hand and the viewer was on."

Mary:

"We have many issues that need to be discussed many of them pertain to earth others are regarding changes that need to be made in here. Earth is where we will begin. There must be change and it must be now there is too much hate to many killings and this must stop. Man must see where hi s destiny lies. If he does not stop thinking only about himself his wants and his needs. Lust, greed, insensitivity, aggression, deprivation, insolence, rape, murder, obscenities, pornography, to mention only a few on a long list of injustices being done to people on earth, add malice, starvation, war and immorality, adultery, stealing, lying, cruelty, destruction of the planet, devastation to the young. All this suffering must stop! The innocent have endured too much pain and anguish, my heart is broken for the mothers and fathers of the children who suffer and cry in the night because of their hunger, because they have nowhere to lay their head to sleep, no medicine to ease their pain. I cry for those that fail and fall into the hands of evil, recklessness, carelessness, abuse and hopelessness. This must change. It is time for a more loving, caring people. I watch as the churches close their doors and the gambling casinos flourish. Men of our Lord entrusted with the spiritual life and faith of the members of their congregation that have betrayed the sacred trust bestowed upon them and use that trust to pursue the evils of their own will, sexual abuse of the children God so loves. These men hide in the shadow of Satan while outwardly gaining the trust of those they are about to destroy. They have helped to destroy the church by destroying the faith people once had in them. To scar a child's heart and plant the seed of fear into their mind that will last a lifetime is the most tragic betrayal to the Lord himself. The whole community no longer has faith in their church or those that administer it. The eye will never look upon these men as just and loving. The trust is no longer binding and the soul is consumed by fear of these holy leaders. There is no place to sit beside the Lord for these sinners."

Sharon:

"Mary sat with her head bent in sadness as she thought for a moment."

Mary:

" People no longer believe that their injustices will have a price and will have to be paid for in an eternity, pictures drawn by their own hand, words written in their own book by their own actions and deeds. What they do today will be shown like a film in a projector. They most definitely will read what they wrote in their book of life. Peoples' fears should not be about the end of times on earth, but about their new beginning after death. They must ask themselves at what level will I spend eternity".

"It is our belief that a messenger is our last hope for mankind. I'm not sure that with even a glimpse into heaven they will change, but at least we will have tried to give them a chance at eternal happiness. They are all our fathers' children and he loves them all and wants them to be happy, but eternal happiness also has a price of love and obedience. Without love and obedience, justice must be handed down.

Earth now has the ability to send our message around the world for all to see and hear. They have the technology to reach every leader in every country of the world. What these leaders choose to do with this information is their own choice. Whether they use this information for peace or for their own power to control, their destiny is in their own hands. Zepherus will speak to the messenger regarding leadership around the world. He and his committee have been working on their message to send to earth with the messenger. Zepherus, would you please take the floor?"

Zepherus:

"It is my honor to tell the messenger of our truths regarding the leaders of the world, whether it is governmental or religious. Law and order are necessary in any society but law and order does not mean control over a persons' mind or rights as a human being. A leader should protect each individual that they represent, whether it is a man or woman or child. No one is going to have to fight for their freedom if they are already free. Our committee has compiled viewing matter for the messenger. This matter will be discussed at the end of the meeting."

Mary:

" As you entered everyone was given an agenda. On the cover there is a list of codes. We will address each issue by code and there is a viewer at your disposal if you need to view any part of the meeting or want to discuss an issue, you need to enter the code and you will be called upon. Your microphone is activated when you are notified that you are up next to speak. You may remain seated at that time.

If visual material is needed, slip the code into the viewer say the word view and all available material will be shown to you. The next issue is regarding the children that have crossed over.

Tasari has brought this issue to my attention after her return with her charge and with so many young dying, and not having a familiar person to greet them on their arrival causes them much stress. We would like to eliminate this as much as possible. Tasari will address this issue of the children crossing over and form a committee to correct these children's needs".

Tasari:

"Thank you Mary, it is good to be back and to join you at conference. I am very thankful to be able to help with this assignment. It is an issue that is very close to my heart.

My charge on earth this time was a little six year old girl that passed over and there was someone familiar to meet her. But many of the children are not as fortunate. They have no one on this side to greet them. Up until now, when a child passed over, there was always someone to greet them, usually a grandparent or an aunt or uncle, someone they knew and recognized. If they did not have someone then Jesus was there to meet with a child that was alone to comfort them but children's lives are more complicated these days. They understand more and are in tune to the emotions of their loved ones.

Many of these children have died a horrible death at the hands of strangers. They were kidnapped and murdered some were never found by their parents and lost forever, some died of fatal diseases, in car accidents, poisonings, fires, drowning, and beatings at the hand of a parent or guardian. These children are terrified and the pain they feel for their parents is unbearable for them.

I would like to find a quicker way to process these children and send them back to visit with their loved ones. I believe it is important for the child to communicate to their loved ones, to let them know that they are safe and have brought all the love in their heart with them. They need to be able to show the parent that they are still alive in their spirit and will see them again someday so the parent may find some comfort in the child's rebirth to the other side. It will not stop the parent's pain, only time will help to heal and put that pain in a different perspective, but it will help the child knowing they at least said goodbye and let their loved one know they still now and always carry them in their heart. It is my belief that if we could assign a supporter and send the child back within the course of a twenty-four hour period earth time, they will adjust to their new life here quicker and with more ease. We will need a guide to return with the child and make the child's plea heard and known to the parent. The child must believe that they have brought comfort to those they love and left behind. We have lost so many children to the other side because they refused to pass over when they were supposed to.

I would like to ask Jacodia to join in this assignment and organize a group of guides to return with the children and help them to communicate with their loved ones through their dreams. She was in charge of the children's division prior to her last tour of earth and has much insight to their needs. We don't want to lose any of these children and leave them to wander the earth in their spirit form because of their fears of crossing over and leaving their parents to suffer. We need to be able to make a promise to the child that they may return to see their loved one again."

Sharon:

"Jacodia stood as she accepted the assignment".

Jacodia:

"I will be honored to work on the project with you. I will assemble a group within a few days and begin the project immediately. I to, find this to be a very necessary installation into the children's division. We will prepare the supporter as soon as the child begins ascension. This way they will be able to be there and make the child aware that they will be able to return to comfort their loved ones. Another issue regarding children is the teenager's levels. Up until now the two levels have been sufficient, but with so many teen's committing violent crimes these days, I think we need an additional level for those teens that do not have any chance at rehabilitation due to the extent of their crimes and the circumstances surrounding the crimes they have committed. A review of each child, their home life and environment must be made, not only the crime will be judged. Their remorsefulness must be taken into consideration.

Level A will be for those that have made the right decisions when the evil one approached them and turned away from the temptation to do wrong. These children weren't always perfect and they made wrong choices some of the time. As all children do. But they knew the choices were wrong and asked for God's forgiveness in doing wrong and His help in doing right.

Level B will be for the child that willfully followed the wrong path, but after searching their heart asked for forgiveness. Their wrong doings were more serious than Level A and time must be spent in the awareness section. But, they can graduate to the higher levels once they have paid the penalty for their disobedience to God.

Level C. These children are not capable of remorse. They are Satan's children. Murder and rape, violence and hate are what live in their heart. They will never seek forgiveness, for they truly love the evil they do. They will be committed to Level C for eternity.

I would like to adjust these levels and incorporate Level C as a separate level for those unable to graduate to a higher level.

My work with the teenagers has been very successful in the past. I would like very much to form a team and continue in this area."

Mary:

"Thank you Tasari and Jacodia., I have much faith in your ability to adjust this situation. We will speak later at the second half of conference once the messenger returns from the levels.

The pollution and destruction of the earth is another issue that must be addressed to the messenger. We must try to find a way for the offenders to realize the irreversible effect they are having on earth. We have tried sending extreme messages to earth without success in the recent past and present, hurricanes, tsunamis, fires, mud slides, tornados, earthquakes and extreme hot and extreme cold temperatures around the globe. Nothing seems to make anyone understand that these are warning signs.

Issias, I know of the work you and your committee has done in the past to improve the quality of life on earth. I would like you to continue in this area and try to find some solution for the messenger to take back with her."

Sharon:

"Issias rose to accept Mary's offer. His face was strong and his words were direct as he spoke. His turquoise robe was now worn with a pale green sash and a turquoise rope belt. He stood sturdy and you could hear his commitment to this issue in his voice".

Issias:

"This is a very difficult assignment. Most of the people responsible for the destruction of the planet are the ones who control the world's economy. They call it big business on earth. Their oil companies, paper mills, steel mills and chemical companies deplete the earth's natural resources faster than they can replenish themselves. They cut down the trees in the rain forests, mine the coal from the earth's crust only to burn it and pollute the air. They are draining the oil from the earth to run their machines. They have been given the knowledge to be able to redirect their source of energy use, but they do not listen. The ozone of this planet will vanish before their eyes.

Loss of land mass will occur, temperatures will rise, the oceans will decay and animals will become extinct. The world's food supply will dwindle and starvation and disease will infiltrate every country of the world. No one will be safe. There will be nowhere for anyone to hide. Money, education, politics, all of this will mean nothing. All the manipulating in the world will not save or stop this chain of events that are about to occur.

So man had better take a closer look into himself, his life and his family, because the watch he wears, the car he drives, the house he walks into and hangs up his hat, the bed he sleeps in at night, the boat he takes on vacation, the dinner he eats, the theater he goes to, even the clothes he wears will mean nothing when the lights go out and all production stops. What would it take to save mankind and change the course of events about to begin? Caring, love of thy neighbor, sharing, understanding and selflessness are what is needed.

This must be a world wide effort on man's behalf. It must begin in the home, spread to the neighborhood, the city, the county, the state, the country, the continent and finally the world. Eyes and hearts must be opened. Ar-Kar-ea my friend, I wish to ask you to join me in this effort and have the committee on earth's reconstruction compile an agenda for the messenger to carry back to earth with her. We have worked together on this problem in the past regarding the chemicals being dumped into the water supply, the air and earth itself and have had much success in these areas. The water supply in many areas had been brought back from toxic to normal levels, but in many areas they are beginning to suffer from high bacteria levels again. Man knows of the destruction he is causing but does not take into consideration that he is responsible today for the future of the life of the earth tomorrow those Responsible will someday have to pay for ignoring all the warning signals. I wish to begin working as soon as possible with you on this project".

Sharon:

"Ar-Kar-ea also wore a turquoise robe with a pale green sash and a pale green rope for a belt."

Ar-kar-ea:

"Thank you Issias for calling upon me to join you".

Sharon:

"Issias stood and continued speaking as Ar-Kar-ea returned to her seat."

Issias:

"There is no variation on this demand. The angels of the wind are already prepared to bring down God's wrath. Petarian, the angel of fire, is waiting in the distant sky. When the word is given, he will set free his ball of fire upon the earth. Aquentelo stirs deep within the ocean. In a moments time he will set forth the waves of disaster and when the ocean meets the land, no one will escape his wrath. Laka-dion is perched upon the mountain ready to split open its side and pour out its liquid, one mountain at a time. Sadarian will scatter among the world ice and snow to fall from the sky. His breath will freeze the wind. Alerana, angel of the earth, her dance will set forth the splitting of the ground and her wings will create circles of wind. All that stands in her path will be devoured.

These things come at a time when no one will be aware. Those that believe God's love and in all he created will enter eternity in peace. To those who have caused this destruction, there will be no peace for eternity.

The human's can change what is happening on earth. They must listen to the voices of those who have listened to their guardians and make the necessary changes to protect earth from global warming. The elders of the earth can testify to the fact that the earth's sun has already changed in its effect on mankind. The heat of the sun's rays on the flesh has intensified. Without protection, there is serious burning to the skin. In snow covered areas the melting of the snow from the sun's heat is happening at an extreme rate. All these changes in nature are signs that things must change for the future of life on earth to continue. There have been many endings to life on earth in earth's past, do not hesitate to think that it cannot or will not happen again. These things will come to pass if there is no change. And this is the word the messenger must bring back to earth regarding the environment on earth. Ar-kar-ea, is there anything you would like to speak of at this time?"

Sharon:

"Issias directed his attention to Ar-kar-ea, as she stood to speak Issias returned to his seat."

Ar-kar-ea:

"Thank you Issias, there is much to be said regarding earth's environment beyond the destruction of the elements. There is also human life, animal life, marine life, plants, birds and insects. People must take a look around at what is happening to the living species on the planet. Not only is global warming responsible for the deterioration of the earth but man himself is also responsible. When acres of natural forests are lost because it has the price of a dollar on it, someone will have to pay the equal amount in eternity for this devastation.

The Greater Cumberland Plateau, the Alaskan Rainforest, Yellowstone National Park, Sonora Desert, Puerto Rico, the Arctic Otero Mesa, Mexico, Nicaragua, the Caribbean, Borneo, China, India, Brazil, Columbia, Africa and Australia and from across the United States, to around the world, there is not a nation that is not touched. All of these regions are home to God's creatures. Their demise should be that of a natural order. It should not be man's actions that eliminate or destroy a species.

Alaska is one of the most troubled areas today with the melting of the icebergs, and the summer sea ice, the polar bears cannot survive, although they are strong swimmers, they cannot endure the distance they have to travel between ice float they may become exhausted and drown. Or when the mother becomes so exhausted and starves because she has used up all of her stored body weight she cannot care for her young cubs, causing both mother and babies to starve to death because they cannot search for food. With their habitat being destroyed, they have nowhere to turn. Sea otters, seals, and walruses will all suffer the same fate with the melting ice.

The gray whales, American alligators, Mud turtles, tortoises, Humpback whales, Gulf sturgeon, Puerto Rico's Rock frogs and many more of earth's life will vanish. Such as: the Peninsular big horn sheep, the grey wolf, Florida panthers, Grizzly bears, the Alaskan white spirit bear and caribou, the African Mt. gorillas, Arabian Oryx, Brazil's Golden monkeys, Otero Mesa mule deer and bobcats, India's Bengal Tigers, American elk and wolves etc. With the destruction of the rain forests the habitat of many of our birds are being destroyed and there is nowhere left for these birds to migrate to. Their nesting grounds are disappearing at an alarming rate. With the disappearance of the birds you have an increase in the insect population. Bats that are being killed in the Amazon have wrecked havoc among the banana plantations, the fruit fly, once kept under control by the bats, are now destroying crops. The Bald Eagle, the Yellow Billed Loon, falcons, Tundra Swans, the Pacific Black Brought, Mexico's Spotted Owls and the Red Cockaded Woodpecker are also endangered.

The Rain Forests are being destroyed at the rate of 25-50 acres per minute. This is not justified in any form. What man destroys causes a trickledown effect on what will be destroyed by nature.

We have been watching earth intensely over the last few decades and although there has been some improvement, it is not nearly enough. Our final message to those destroying the earth is to be aware my friends, be truly aware of what eternity has in store for you. Remember God created the Red Cedars, the Giant Sequoias, the Sitka Spruce and every living thing on your planet. Our committee will continue in our efforts to bring a solution to mankind regarding the saving of the planet earth. I can only pray the messenger can make this message clear."

Mary:

"Thank you Issias, and Ar-kar-ea, your knowledge will be very helpful to the messenger on her return. Your message is clear.

Sharon, I am confident that what you have heard will not be difficult for you to make known. Remember what you were told of here today and speak only of that which you have been given knowledge of.

The next issue on the agenda pertains to the suffering on earth to God's children because of the color of their skin or their origin, their religious beliefs or their politics. This is the most complex of all issues. We here in heaven do not comprehend the meaning of racism, we do not discriminate. There is no such word in our dialect to describe such an action. Are-lea has recently returned from earth and her major concern is that of the injustices being done to people because of who they are where they come from the color of their skin or what their beliefs are. Mans features and colors were not created as a judgment man was created in the image of God and as he traveled to new areas of the earth his features and skin had to adjust to the change in the climate they were living. Those living in the hottest and sunniest regions had to have a courser a darker color of skin to protect them from their environment. Those living in open regions where the glare of the suns light reflects from the elements such as snow had developed a protective shape to their eyes over time. The milder regions where the climate was mixed with hot and cold developed a fair coloring to their skin. This was a natural development for mankind. It does not reflect on his intelligence his strength or his superiority. All of mankind is born with intellect it is only knowledge he needs to learn. Does man not understand that these are all of Gods children that in his eyes they are all brothers and sisters with only one father and that if they hurt one of his children they are hurting him too. No one wants to have someone hurt their child this also pertains to God.

Are-lea would you like to give the messenger any advice to take back with her regarding this issue?"

Sharon:

"Are-lea stood and directed her attention to me. She wore a violet robe with a white sash and a violet rope for a belt her hair was a golden red and her eyes were a deep warm brown. She had the beauty of an angel and you could see her tenderness on her face."

Are-lea:

"Thank you Mary I have spent several years with my charge on earth and I could not protect him against the suffering he had to endure. He watched as his wife each one of his three children his neighbors his family members and his friends died of aids hunger disease or violence. His government did little if anything to help them. His village was destroyed and all of his belongings were lost. He was sent to a camp where food and medical assistance were also scarce but his faith never wavered. He prayed for God to help the children and their mothers to protect the grandparents and to keep the volunteers that came to the villages and camps safe. He never prayed for his own needs only for forgiveness. He prayed for others that were in need. These people were treated less than human only because of who they are.

I would like to thank you Mary for giving me this opportunity to speak to the messenger I pray our message reaches the hearts of the people on earth these injustices should not be allowed to continue. Man must learn to accept each other and not judge one another because of some misguided ideal from the past man must learn to look into a heart look into the eyes of their children. They all love and smile and cry as you do. They all sing songs and pray to God. They all feel pain and have fears. Turn away from hate and judgment let respect and tolerance be your shield against this evil. If man must discriminate, then discriminate against hate, poverty, murders, thieves, rapists, drug dealers, and all evil. These are the ways things should be. These are the words for you to bring back to earth with you to help mankind soften their hearts.

Do not judge everyone because of a few. Open your hearts and your eyes. Look beyond what you were taught and see through clearer eyes. Do not judge a person who has less than you because there is always going to be someone who has more than you. They will be judging you. When you go to work, talk to your co-workers. Ask them about their child, about their wife, about their dreams and about their life and you will see it is not much different then what your own life is.

If you find yourself in a position where someone is being disrespectful of another person because of their color or their race, stand up for your beliefs and do not turn away from them. Sometimes all it takes is to say a kind word to make someone realize that not everyone agrees with the way they think or act towards another human being. " I do not believe in being prejudice against a whole race because of the actions of a few. There is always good and bad in every race and most people, if given a chance, will treat you with respect if they are also treated with respect."This response is not a challenge, it is only a statement. It is a sign of good will to all. You must make man understand that no one has the right to impose their ideals or their lifestyles on anyone else. To respect someone's traditions and way of life will bring peace to the world.

Thank you Mary for this opportunity to have this message returned to earth. Mankind is capable of much more compassion than what he gives. He needs to understand what is not acceptable in God's eyes. I would like to take a moment to say thank you to Sharon for accepting the responsibility as the messenger. Although it is not an easy task, I am sure you will express our thoughts clearly and bring them to man's attention."

Sharon:

"I stood as I thanked Are-lea. I told her I would do everything possible to express her concerns on this issue upon my return to earth. I sat again as Mary rose once again to speak."

Mary:

"Thank you,Are-lea and Sharon. I also have something to add to

37

Are-lea's concerns and this has very much become a world- wide problem. Acceptance of another countries religious beliefs, language, dance, food, and political stance are progress, as long as it does not interfere with the peace of another country, should be upheld. Many countries have developed technologies useful to the world. This is called progress. But many countries do not find technology necessary. They are perfectly happy living a simpler life and do not want or are not ready for change. This must be their choice.

Tyranny and oppression are not considered choices, they are control. These tyrants use death and violence, poverty and propaganda against their people to keep them in order. They, on the other side of the spectrum, do need help and it is the duty of the world to intervene. But intervention should only occur when helping humanity is the issue. Politics or the control of a country's finance's is an unacceptable reason to intervene. You cannot justify war for profit. Nor can you justify killing for control. The taking of an innocent life is unacceptable no matter what the circumstance and to take a life in the name of the Lord is unforgivable. God is not violent. God represents love and peace. There is no killing of the innocent that will go unpunished. Thou shall not kill does not mean it is alright to kill some of the time."

Sharon:

"Mary turned as she readjusted the viewer to change the format."

Mary:

"Many of you here today have spent the last few earth decades with your chargers you have watched as they have endured great happiness and great sorrows. I would like to give you an opportunity to express any concerns you may have regarding your charge and if you have any suggestions that the messenger may take back with her that could make a positive impact and help to better one's life. I know that there is much evil that walks the earth and causes much pain to the innocent, unaware people. Hopefully, if they become aware of what is happening to them they may be able to better prepare themselves against evil."

Sharon:

"Kardarian rose to speak. He wore an aqua colored robe with a coral sash and an aqua color rope for a belt. His hair was a chestnut brown and his eyes were a light hazel. He was tall and his figure was lean. He had a smile that could melt your heart."

Kardarian:

"My concerns are not of a world problem. It is not a political or an

38

environmental problem it is, however, regarding the evil that exists in every neighborhood, in every city and causes much pain and anguish.

My charge on earth this time was as evil a person that could walk the earth. He was evil from the time he could begin thinking, walking, and talking. I could not reach this charge under any circumstance. My whispers fell on deaf ears, but he did not hesitate to listen to Satan's cries to do evil.

It began with his sibling's. He accused them of doing wrong deeds that he himself had done and laughing as they tried to defend themselves against his wrong doings. He would hide himself in a doorway and listen and jump up and down rubbing his hands together as his sibling was being punished by being hit with a strap or a switch. As he grew older the torturing of animals was where he got his next thrills. He would contain them and poke them with sticks or burn them with lit cigarettes. He loved the control he had over these animals. It gave him sexual pleasure to watch them suffer. When he was done with them he would open the cage and watch as they tried to crawl out to safety.

He could never keep a friend when he was in school because he would frighten them with his talk of killing and maiming, control and torture. No one wanted to associate with him. He loved the look of fear in their eyes and the way they wrinkled their forehead and turned away from him only to have to look back again. At this he would smile and point his finger at them.

As he grew to adulthood, so did his evil. His family wanted nothing to do with him. His mother and father feared him. He would harass them and their neighbor's. He harassed his father to the point that his father took a gun and shot him. But nothing stopped him. His father went to jail and he walked out of court laughing.

He abused drugs and sold them to supply his own habit. He met a young girl who had an abusive relationship with her adoptive family. He got her on drugs and abused her too. She got pregnant and eventually they had three children. By this time she joined him in selling drugs. The children were taken away from them and they both did their time in jail. After he got out they had permission to take the children for a day. They never brought them back. They took the children and ran to another state. Nothing had changed there. He began his harassment of his neighbors, abused his own children, and kept his wife supplied in drugs as well as himself. He had his girlfriends on the side while his wife worked. When she would confront him he would threaten to kill her. She was under his control and believed she could not live without him. He had her convinced that she couldn't trust anyone so she was kept isolated. She had no friends and he had destroyed what little relationship she had with her family. They moved from apartment to apartment because of his stalking other tenant's children and harassing the adults. He would always accuse the other party of doing him wrong. They would move and it would start over again. They finally had the opportunity to buy a house on a close knit, friendly street, and he did. At first everything seemed fine. The unaware neighbors welcomed them with open arms. They were invited to backyard parties and picnics. Soon this was to become a nightmare. His true inner side began to show when he began playing his music. The words were not something anyone wanted their children to listen to it not only had curse words but the contents were so vile the adults took offense of it. The music was so loud you could hear it all the way down the street it literally shook the walls of the people next door to them. When asked to turn the music down he turned it up, he was like a defiant child and the neighbors were dumb founded.

The housing inspectors began to show up because of the complaints made by this new neighbor. He walked around with a camcorder and took pictures up and down the street at first he took pictures of the houses then he would sit on his porch and record every move the neighbors made. That led to him recording their children, making verbal comments and sexual gestures.

His wife turned away from the friendship of her new neighbors in defense of her husband saying that's just the way he was. This man would set off fireworks call the police and accuse someone else of doing it he would throw trash into the street and onto some ones lawn or sidewalk. He got so bad he began to take his penis out and wave at the women and young girls as they walked home from school. Parents were enraged the children were terrified and husbands were ready to kill him the neighborhood was frantic. The police were of little help they had more important issues to deal with then a neighborhood feud. By the end of summer the neighborhood had five households had orders of protection, against this man. It took all this time for the neighbors to realize that this was his intent all along, anger the neighbors and keep his wife and children isolated, as to keep them under his control.

I watched as the guardians, protected their charges as they whispered in their ear and helped any real violence from happening, the guardians whispered for them to not wish revenge on your enemy but pray to God to help that person to change. Of course that person did not change he was evil and Satan protected him but the prayers helped to take away the anger that had grown inside of everyone's heart and replace it with an inner peace and self control. The neighbors got together and agreed to ignore this mans, actions against them and to act as though he never existed, his wife and children also became a part of this action because they could not break away from his evilness. One night this charge was found on the other side of town lying in the street in a pool of blood with a bullet in his head.

When the news became available to the public there was no one there to mourn him or to Comfort his family there was only praise to God for taking him away. This is the payment you receive from Satan for living in his shadow. So no matter who is causing you this pain let it be a co-worker a neighbor a relative or a so called friend turn away from them and try to ignore their action it will not make them happy because what they want is to see your reaction your anger your pain. This would give a sense of control regarding the situation, evil needs a reaction to an action otherwise it means nothing to the performer."

Sharon:

"Kardarian then sat and arrange his papers. He had a look of thoughtfulness across his face as he looked my way."

Mary:

"Thank you Kardrian for this informative speech regarding your last charge I am sure it was good to return home. And I am sure that this charge has already been sent to the appropriate level to spend his eternity. Evil acts that are inflicted upon a person will not go unanswered in eternity these deeds will pay a high price to the perpetrator, let it be known, acts of evil toward man for self pleasure will reap a severe punishment for eternity. Satan's children are not welcome at the Lords gate.

Maralisea I see that you have entered your name to speak, please stand and discuss your issues at this time."

Sharon:

"Maralesia wore a lavender color robe with a plum color sash and a lavender rope as a belt. Her hair was a deep brown and it lay long down her back with a plum color ribbon tied through it. She had deep brown eyes that matched her hair and a soft glow to her face, she was beautiful and she had a look of confidence and poise about her as she stood to speak."

Maralesia:

"My charge on earth this last tour, was born into a wealthy family, both her father and mother were famous in the motion picture industry.

She was the center of everyone's attention as a child, and what a sweet child she was, polite and respectful to everyone, but as she grew older her parents began to have problems, they were apart most of the time due to their jobs, and we when she was six years old her parents divorced. She no longer had the stability of a home and family she was left with nannies and housekeepers and was shipped to one parent to other for summers and holiday vacations.

Although her parents both loved her they were caught up in their own lives, work, exercise, dating, traveling, shopping, parties and premiers, all of the things that kept her separated from love, kisses, hugs and story books, help with homework, having someone there to recognize the tear in her eye or the look of sadness on her face, there was no one to smile at the picture she colored or the baseball she hit. When she was sick and alone no one was by her side to comfort her. The nanny put her to bed, the cook fixed her meals and the chauffeur drove her to school. She was alone and her life was surrounded by toys, gifts and strangers. By the time she was fifteen she pretty well learned to accept her life the way it was, mom had remarried and dad had gone through a few relationships. Still no one wanted the responsibility of being the parent, mom tried to act her like best friend, dad still thought of her as a child.

Her friends at school were friendly but they lived so far away she never had a chance to visit them on a regular basis. She was a good student in school and joined the glee club, there she met a boy she began to like and he was quick to return his feelings, he too had lived a similar life and was lonely but this boy was a little more experienced in the world. He had taken drugs, drank alcohol, and experienced with sex. As always there was no one there to talk to or for this child to ask for guidance from. She was on her own. She thought it would be O.K to smoke some "pot" one night when this boy stopped by. And she did no big deal she thought everyone at school talks about it all the time. From there she went and tried drinking alcohol. She thought this was great the loneliness wasn't as severe anymore. She was high on drugs, under the influence of alcohol one night and had sex. She was only sixteen years old. By now her grades began to fall, she dropped out of the glee club, and quit the softball team. This child that had once loved school was now missing more days then she was attending. Her mother became aware of her problems with school after running into one of her teachers while shopping. When she approached her daughter at home that evening the child started screaming at her mother to leave her alone, she questioned her mother as to why after all these years was she concerned about her, after all she told her mom, you were never here before.

I tried to protect her from these evils but her pain was too much for her, this beautiful lonely girl, left the house got on her motorcycle and drove it off a cliff. The police said at the rate of speed she was going she could not negotiate the curve. This accident left two parents devastated and a child dead. What would have prevented all of this, two loving parents that cared for each other and took the time to look at the true values in their lives with all their money they could not find happiness because they are always looking for more then what they already have. Respect for one another's feelings, faithfulness, loyalty "Love" a kind word, protection, when a person can say I love my husband, or I love my wife, when the other is not around to hear it. There is no greater respect for a person. I often over heard a man or woman speak badly about their spouse the minute they were away from one another. What kind of a person would violate such a trust my message for you to bring back to earth is for humans to try to remember that nothing in life is easy, this includes marriage, but if humans would stop and think of all of the consequences they might try a little harder to get along."

Sharon:

"Maralesia took a seat as she entered her papers into the viewer Mary then stood and addressed the audience."

Mary:

"Thank you Maralisea for this reflection of your last charge we were all saddened by these events, married couples must stop being so angry with each other, and never put someone else before their spouse, this includes friends, family members, co-workers. They must remember that they both are individuals with their own thoughts and ways of doing things. Let each other have their own time separate from another, just because one spouse doesn't want to do everything the other wants to do it doesn't mean they don't love the other spouse it only means they don't want to do that exact same thing at the exact same time and that's all right. They have to learn to make time for the things they do like to do together. When they find themselves having a problem about something, make time to sit down and discuss it. Don't just throw accusations at one another. This only causes hurt feelings and anger. Listen to what's being said to each other. Children accuse and blame. Adults need to talk and adjust a situation. The heart always starts out as a whole in any marriage, but lies and the loss of trust cause that whole to be chipped away at. Sooner or later there is nothing left and the heart is left a cold empty shell. Then loneliness begins to set in. Don't allow this to happen to you or your spouse. A smile or a kiss or a sweet word or just saying I love you before work or at the dinner table can make a world of difference in your loved ones life. It fills the heart with love rather than loneliness.

I tell you these things to help these people work out their relationships, because the pain they are causing to one another and to their children will not be forgotten when they reach eternity. They should stop looking at what only makes their self happy and begin thinking of others as well. The level you will spend in eternity is the level you are building today. The pain you cause today will not be forgotten tomorrow.

Cara-dari, I see that you have placed your name on the list. Please stand and express your thoughts regarding your issues."

Sharon:

"Cara-dari stood and smiled as she began to speak she wore a yellow robe with white trim and a yellow rope as a belt. Her hair was golden and worn long and flowing down her back. She had light green eyes and flowers lay in a wreath upon her head."

Cara-dari:

"Thank you, Mary, I am so grateful to have this opportunity to be able to express my thoughts on some of the things I found to be important on this last journey to earth. I know there are many changes that need to be made, and there is much evil, but the things I wish to speak of are not of an evil nature.

My duty this time on earth was to determine whether the human race was capable of compassion towards one another. This duty brought me to every corner of the earth and what I found were many acts of kindness, love, thoughtfulness, sacrifice, heroics, consideration, concern and helpfulness towards their fellow man on earth. These people, I believe, are earths' angels. Many of these people put the lives of strangers before their own life. In the midst of war I found heroes, both men and women, who stepped in and protected a wounded soldier and brought them to safety, the soldier who stood his ground so others may get to safety, and the soldier that made the greatest sacrifice of all and gave his life for his fellow soldiers without a thought of himself. This kind of bravery and sacrifice is for those special few that carry the Beta in their soul. Unconsumed by self and overflowing with compassion.

In the Far East I found news reporters searching through rubble trying to find survivors after a devastating earthquake. Let it be a hurricane in the

Caribbean, flooding in the United States, starvation in Africa or the war in the Middle East, these brave men and women put their lives on the line, not only for a story but to carry the truth to those around the world. The rescue worker is always there to help save the lives of people in danger or in need. They are there to help someone that has fallen off a cliff or survivors of a ship wreck that were stranded after their ship sank. The helping hand of a stranger reaching down to bring them to safety is an act of bravery, an act of caring. Many of those who ran to someone's assistance gave their own life while saving someone in need. The volunteers and rescue workers that give of them self to help others that need a caring hand, let it be an animal, a child or an adult that finds themselves without someone to turn to there is that special person willing to give of them self without asking for a reward of any kind , Earth angels, yes. The strong arms of a firefighter as he carried a mothers' child to her open outstretched arms moments before a building collapses behind them, or to the firefighter who gives his life without thought or hesitation to protect his fellow man, the police officer that looks with caring eyes and has the sound of compassion in his voice as he consoles the victim of a crime. The sheriff that gives his life to protect the citizens he has never met, from a gun wielding criminal. The state trooper that holds the hand of an accident victim until their last breath and then personally visit the home of the next of kin to break the news of their loved ones accident and console them with kindness and compassion. It's the one step above and beyond. Earth angel's yes.

I remember well this widow she had little money, but always had enough food to feed anyone who came into her home. If someone were in need of somewhere to stay, she always found a place for them to sleep, if just for the night or for six months, if you were in need she was there to help. These people that came to her always knew they would be provided with a warm bed and food to eat and kindness. She asked for nothing in return, only that you thank the Lord for what little they did have.

An elderly woman's car had a flat tire on her return trip after visiting her mother in a nursing home, from another state. It was dark and cold and she was in an area unfamiliar to her. There she stood, tire jack in hand and not a clue as to how to use it. Fifty cars must have passed her by and not one of them attempted to slow down to help her. Frightened and alone, tears began to well up in her eyes, Oh Lord please help me, she called out and with a look over her shoulder she saw a woman approach the car. She was a little woman, probably in her early thirties, much younger than her sixty five years. The woman had the most beautiful smile she had ever seen.

She talked a little about the cold and then gave the old woman a candy bar. She then reached for the tire iron and jack, and before she knew it her tire was fixed and she was able to drive the car again. The old woman thanked the girl again and offered her payment for helping her. The girl stood and looked at the old woman for a moment "Isn't that why we're here to help one another and not to look for something in return, this is the lords way. " and she turned with a smile and as quickly as she had appeared she disappeared into the night. The young girl will never be forgotten by the old woman and she tells everyone she meets about the kindness of this stranger that entered her life one lonely night on a dark highway.

When a crisis occurs there is always the neighbor who without hesitation runs out anytime day or night to help offering a ride or just a shoulder to lean on but you know without a doubt that that this person will be there for whoever is in need, let it be an elderly neighbor, a child in need after a fall off their bike, a friend that needs help caring for her terminally ill husband, or running to the aid of a friend who's husband has just died of a massive heart attack in the middle of the night, and then spends the rest of the night serving coffee to friends that gather to consol their friend. Earth angle's" yes ".

I watched closely to a woman her husband had been diagnosed with cancer, she watched as this once strong, independent man filled with laughter and humor, who loved life, his wife, his family, and his friends. Who welcome strangers and loved the children. I watched as she cared for him and loved him as this terrible disease wrecked havoc within his body and drained every ounce of life from him, she never hesitated to clean up after him, dress his wounds, bathe him, and love him. She kept her tears out of sight from him and always showed him her smile. She helped him to keep his dignity by agreeing to his wishes, and sometimes when she knew it may not have been what was right for him, she quietly got him to change his mind. She remained brave and strong for him until he took his last breath.

One of earth's angel's yes.

I found much kindness from doctors who truly cared for their patients, and over looked their short comings, they saw beyond the physical aspect of a person, and understood their fears and weaknesses. They help those that are self absorbed and sympathize with their circumstances they help those that don't take their illnesses seriously enough by explaining the consequences to them. They do all the right things and leave the rest up to the patient himself. They do not judge, they do not anger they only try to heal. Earth's angel's yes."

I found earth angels on many door steps on earth, the nurses that dedicate their lives to making other people's lives comfortable, the ambulance attendant and the paramedic that works diligently to save a life, the teacher that finds a way to help a child that needs him or her the most and recognizes a child in need, bad behavior or not being able to concentrate may be related to abuse in the home, a distrust or fear of authority is a sigh of being abused by those with authority in their lives. A child cannot trust any adult if they fear the adults in their own home.

If a parent strikes a child how do they know that a stranger wouldn't do the same, if a parent tells them they are stupid and useless, fat or ugly, why would someone else not think the same of them? After all if you can't trust your parents, those that are supposed to love you who can you trust? A kind word, knowing when someone needs a little extra attention, being aware of the fact that a child just isn't getting what they need in their lives, a little love and attention can go a long way with these children. One of earth's angel's yes.

My journey has brought me many riches from earth and I will keep them in my heart forever.

Thank you Mary for allowing me to share the beauty of these humans I have seen on earth."

Sharon:

"Cara-dari closed her folder and took her seat she wrapped her arms around her folder and bowed her head in prayer."

Mary:

"Thank you Cara-dari, you have giving us hope in the people of earth. I too know that there are many more of earth angels that add quality to someone else's life. They give of themselves to make life easier for others. There is a special place in heaven that awaits these caring, loving humans Sharon, the message I wish for you to carry back with you is the word of Gods' love towards their fellow man, look beyond what they see only with their eyes and look into someone's heart. Their own heart must tell them truth their faith must guide them in the right direction, but not to be fooled by evil, be aware of those around them and do not become a victim because of their kindness.

Listen closely to the words of the angle that speaks of the lords words, open your heart and mind to the kindness of your waiter or hair dresser, your child's teacher, the bus driver and aide, to the phone operator that is trying to assist you or the secretary trying to understand what kind of help you need, have compassion for the clerk or cashier that has five other customers ahead of you and is trying to please everyone at the same time. Be patient with the parking attendant, he has enough stress with the responsibility of taking care of your car let alone some one that treats him with disrespect because they're in a hurry or is angry at something else that happened to them an hour before and thinks it's O.K to talk down to someone they'll probably never see again this is not acceptable behavior, it has a trickle down affect that affects every person that comes in contact with every person they meet that day. Let's see how many people can just one miserable person make unhappy in the course of one day? The parking attendant, the fifty or so customers he had after that, the five or more people that every one of those customers may encounter. Let's see. Now we're topping two hundred and fifty people that were unhappy just because one person had a bad day. Think about your postal carrier take into consideration the weather, their age, all the walking they must do the weight of the mail bag, animals that hate them and traffic, a polite hello and a friendly smile is like a thank you card.

I remember a guardian once telling me of a charge that was born with a horrible deformity he lived in a remote part of the world where strangers seldom ventured but this one day a social worker traveling with a health agency came into this village and saw this child that was an outcast. The adults shunned him and the children ridiculed him the only ones he had to love him were his family. Well this stranger took his pictured and mailed it to a doctor friend of hers in the United States this doctor got a team together and had this child brought over to the states to have surgery. Everyone involved volunteered their time and expense to help save this little child. The boy was away from home for over a year and he spent this time with a social worker that doubled as a foster mother she cared for him and loved him as though he were her own. When the time came for him to return home she shed tears of sorrow along with her tears of joy. The team of doctors and nurses involved in his surgeries grew to love this little boy too and after a series of successful surgeries that promised a happier life for this child it meant he would soon be returning home. They showered him with lots of gifts love and good by kisses. Did any of these people have to give of themselves? No but they truly are angels of the earth.

Think of the cook in a hot steamy kitchen trying to prepare fifty meals and has one customer that has to be rude to the waitress because his steak is under cooked and begins yelling at her what happens next, well she is going to go into the kitchen all upset because someone yelled at her and she is going to upset the cook that has no idea as to what's going on because he has five dinners coming up and he is trying to make them perfect now his concentration is broken he tells the waitress to wait a minute she is in a huff the manager is now in a huff the other cooks are distracted the fine tuned mechanism that runs the kitchen is now off set and why because one customer had to be rude and obnoxious to the waitress. Be polite be kind a "could you please help me" will go a long way to help keep the day in order.

Do you think for a moment that these kindnesses will be forgotten or go unrewarded for every kindness is written in your book of life every smile every time you volunteer to help a stranger in need without looking for praise for yourself with every charitable and noble act you perform you are giving praise to the lord. You are helping to do the lords work for him, remember too for every unkind act for every evil act for every selfish self serving act you commit these acts will also be recorded in your book of life. These acts give praise to Satan not to the lord so be aware of your eternity be aware of as to whom you want to be loyal to. Jacardian, I see that you have entered your name to speak. We have spoken before and I am aware of your thoughts please speak freely as to the depths of evil you have encountered on your last tour of earth. Sharon please listen closely to what's being said and be aware of this evil you are to hear of next, because on your journey through the levels you will encounter all of these evils."

Sharon:

"Mary then sat and directed her attention to Jacardian. Jacardian stood and looked at Samarious and me, he was a handsome angel with shoulder length auburn hair his eyes were the color of the deepest green in the sea. He wore a deep green robe with a pale green sash and a deep green rope as a belt. He was of medium height with a slender build."

Jacardian:

"My duty this time was to assess earth because of the fact the lower levels are the levels that are filling up at an alarming rate much quicker than any of the other levels. The question that needed to be answered is why. So my journey began. The facts are clear it is pure evil.

My tour of earth was not that of a nature I would want anyone on earth to have to endure yet many are suffering at an unprecedented rate."

Sharon:

"As Jacardian stood and spoke his words were calm and clear as though he did not want anyone to ever forget what he had to say."

Jacardian:

"Unlike Cara-daris journey that sent her on a search to find the good the angels of the earth my mission was to find where Satan was hiding and to see how his power had control over the humans and to what length they would go to enable him to grow and to survive. There are many forms of evil on earth and these evils grow stronger every day. I have seen evil acts from every corner of the globe from the least sever to the most horrific in nature.

I have been a beta from the beginning of time and I have seen humans with depraved indifference to life. From the beginning of mankind we expected this behavior once man lost his paradise and had to learn how to survive on his own. We have seen war and devastation an attempt at genocide. The uncivilized world would rape and pilfer everything in sight. Man was cruel and unforgiving in his nature, he was savage and predatory. But man has progressed and knowledge of what is right and what is wrong moral or immoral has been implanted in his brain he is no longer uncivilized by nature he is though uncivilized by choice.

Greeting Sharon, I welcome you. Your message of our levels will not hasten the true evil doers to change their ways. Their minds are eroded by their thoughts, by their actions. But, I pray, that it will help to prevent those that are beginning to have depraved thoughts to turn away from Satan and to look for the lords help. All humans must take a deep look into their own mind they must search out and destroy Satan's manipulation. Parents must watch their children carefully, and try to protect them from Satan's influence. Teach them prayer at an early age, guide them morally and spiritually. Tell them who God is and what he wants and expects from them so they may enter the gates of heaven and live eternity in peace, surrounded by love and joy.

I am sending a warning to all those that lie and manipulate and cause an unjustified consequent, pain or anguish, to the innocent. To those that maim and kill God's creatures just because they want to. To those that have uncontrollable anger, and vent that anger at anyone they seemed fit to, without any regard for that person's life or health or emotional being. To those of you that abuse your wife, husband or child, physically or mentally, to the men of God that have broken their vows and brought harm to any member of their congregation. To the child molesters that take away a child's innocents and scar their mind and cause so much pain for the rest of their life. To the drug dealer, that willfully destroys another person's life by offering to introduce them to paradise but sends them into a life time of hell. Then sits back and buy cars, jewelry, and toys. This is the price you put on a person's life? Do you know how you are going spend your eternity? You will soon know exactly how and where you stand and you won't be driving a big car or staying in a big house, wearing expensive jewelry, or flashing a lot of money.

To the drug user that steal's to support their habit, or sells their body for a fix and does unscrupulous acts just to put a drug into their body. You who have destroyed your relationships with all family and friends, you who made the conscience decision to do whatever it is you do without regard for anyone else. You will lie, you will cheat, and you will steal to get whatever it is that you want. Face it now or face it when you die. The choice to change is yours. To the thief, you take what you want from who you want to take something from, you don't care that someone has worked hard for what they have, you don't care that the money that you stole from that old woman was supposed to feed her for the month, pay her rent, buy her medicine, and pay her bills. You don't care that this woman is now terrified to go outside the door, she is even terrified to answer the phone and you also don't care that the jewelry you took from that young woman was the only thing she had of her husband that was killed in the war, and what about the food you stole from work, did you think stealing from work didn't make a difference? It all counts it all makes a difference.

To you the adulterer or to you the mistress do you think that you can cheat and sneak or hide and no one can see ,do you think this is a harmless act that this betrayal is forgivable when your spouse discovers this betrayal what will you say to her when look into her or his eyes and see the sorrow or the anger you know that your relationship will never be the same the trust when lost can never return and the love once felt so innocent and true will be buried in the heartache. She may forgive you because she loves you but she will never forget the pain.

To the husband that leaves his wife for another woman or to the woman that leaves her husband for another man how can you just make someone feel as they've been thrown out just like the trash being set to the curb. To cause a heart so much pain do you think this betrayal will go unanswered, of course not.

To the victims of these perpetrators you may not see your justice on earth but you will surly see justice handed down in heaven.

To those who have allowed greed to infest your life take time to think of the homeless person that wraps rags around his hands and feet to keep warm.

And to you the person so full of jealousy and hate for those that have more than what you have, it fills your days and nights with bitterness and anger. Try to realize not everyone can be the prettiest or the richest or the smartest instead of wallowing in self pity try to find something better about yourself that you can excel in the face of a jealous person is like that of a hidden demon.

One of the most unforgivable crimes comes from the betrayal of those in a political or a position of those in authority. The politician that takes money from the criminals to further his or her career or to put money in their own bank accounts or campaign fund uses their power for sexual favors, personal gratification and to feed their ego. Ah do not believe for a moment that there is honor amongst thieves there is only the knowledge that neither of you are trustworthy. When your term is over where will your allies then be? When criminal charges are brought against you do you believe your cohorts will stand behind you or go to prison for you or do you think they may turn states evidence and get a get out of jail free card? Remember judgment is at hand although Cara-dari found many earth angels on the police force I found much corruption. Money, sex, drugs, and power are what fueled these followers of Satan. And who do these people trust, the drug dealers, the pimps the prostitutes? Maybe they trust the guy that's paying them off to turn their backs on the sale of guns their going to make, or maybe they trust the car shop that steals and then sells hot cars to overseas dealers. Oh I know they can trust the guy who runs the little mom and pop shop that they have been extorting money from for the past six years, maybe just maybe they will be able to trust the gang member that they planted evidence on because they wanted him off the streets for a while I am sure they will be able to trust him when he gets out of jail. Change your ways your destiny awaits you.

To those of you that have committed the most violent crime of rape be prepared to pay the highest price for your crime just because you think you have hidden your crime in the shadows of the night in the darkest corners you can hide nothing from your book of life, every moment of your life is recorded every infraction noted when you pass over and are judged your own book will be your judgment.

To the person who so viciously takes the life of another human being with absolutely disregard or thought of pain you so callously inflicted on that person the mental or physical torture this person had to endure will be nothing compared to the eternity you will spend. No amount of begging screaming or pleading will help you there will be no defense in heaven your judgment stands written in your own hand by your own deeds.

A final act of judgment is to those that have no belief in an afterlife no belief in God theirs is probably the most severe of eternal judgment.

I have given insight into your future as the laws of heaven are written all humans must pay their tally at life's end there is no escaping death and no one will ever be aware of that moment in time until they are at heaven's gate asking permission to enter. The way is clear into the Lords house it is simple follow the laws the father given you and repent your sins from the deepest part of your soul. The father loves all of his children and he is a fair and just father you either follow his words or be punished for an eternity.

God gives us a place to go home to after we die we are all his prodigal sons and daughters at what level you will enter eternity is a choice only you can make on earth. My final words for you to bring back to earth with you Sharon is to prepare now before your time on earth is over because then there will be no escaping your judgment. Think about who will remember you after you pass over, will you be a thought in the mind of someone for a day, a week, or for years to come? Will you fill someone's heart with precious memories to comfort them with love or will you be remembered with hate? The choice is yours a thought from those left behind for a moment or a life time. Will they grieve over you or be thankful you are gone?"

Sharon:

"Jacardian then sat and as he looked my way he nodded his head and smiled. "

Mary:

"Sharon, Jacardian has given you an insight as to what you will experience when you journey through the levels. There is much evil to be seen but there will also be much beauty.

The hour has come for us to close this meeting the messenger must soon begin her final steps for her journey through our heaven.

Zepherus I will meet with you and Sharon for one last time before you enter the levels after we have left the arena, please join me at the entrance room to the levels at this time."

Sharon:

"Mary turned her attention away from Zepherus and myself and directed her closing statements to the betas."

Mary:

"We will meet again at the twelfth hour after Zepheru and the

53

messenger has left us, at that time we will discuss the matters regarding heaven.

Thank you all for making our conference a success once again."

Sharon:

"Mary collected her files and she and the betas that sat at her table turned and left the arena. The betas began to talk amongst each other as they left the arena they all smiled and offered their hand in friendship as they greeted one another.

Zepherus then offered me his arm in a gesture for me to follow him I of course followed his lead. We spoke only for a moment as he led me through the exit door of the arena. As we passed through the gateway we entered a room with a desk and a few chairs the room over looked a water fall and you could see a creek and many trees and beautiful flowers."

Zepherus:

"This is Mary's office she conducts all of her business here. I often feel as though earths problems don't even exist when we're sitting discussing a project or an event that's about to take place and after listening to what's going on in the world today I am truly thankful that I am a beta. Sharon I want you to know before we enter the levels and begin our decent what an honor it is to have met you it was not an easy decision choosing a messenger the search was long and the candidates were many but when you were selected we all here knew you were the right choice and now after knowing you it truly pleases me to be a part in your journey. Do not allow any of the things that may happen to you on earth deter you from the path you are taking, the road will be long and your trials many but always remember we are here watching over you."

Sharon:

"At that moment Mary entered the room."

Mary:

"Greetings, Zepherus and Sharon,. I am sorry that we didn't have more time to spend at conference but I know the journey ahead of is long and I didn't want to hold you up any longer then what was necessary. There was so much to be said at conference regarding earth and I did not anticipate it taking up so much of our time. We will continue with conference after you have begun your journey it is upon your return Zepherus that you will be made aware of the changes we wish to make here. It is not necessary at this time for the messenger to be delayed any longer. Sharon, go with Zepherus in peace and in faith and remember at all times no harm will come to you we will be monitoring you very closely on your decent. May peace be with you on your journey."

Sharon:

"Mary gave me a warm hug and clasped Zephyrus's hand. She then exited the room."

Zepherus:

"Take my arm and we shall begin."

Sharon:

"Zepherus took my hand and tucked it tightly in his arm I noticed with amazement as two wings came out from slits in the back of his robe when they were fully opened he led me through a door into a bright light in a moment's time we were standing at the edge of the first level at that point Zepheruses wings folded back beneath his robe once again."

CHAPTER FOUR LEVEL 1

Part A
The Holy

Zepherus:

"This is the first level it is the beginning of our journey this is God's home, it is where the most holy those who lived their lives in honor and praise to the lord sit beside his thrown for eternity they surround him and listen to his wisdom, he speaks of things from the beginning of time to the present at times they laugh with the lord other times they have cried.

The Priests, Ministers, Monks, Moslems, Buddhists, Hindus, Rabbis the cloistered men and women that have dedicated and sacrificed their lives to God because of their love for the lord thy God. For those who believe the truth and what God has told them an eternity will be spent sitting beside him and walking in paradise. For those not willing to believe what they were told will bring them to another part of this level. God loves all of these souls and knows of their dedication and their belief in him and of their love for him but he also expects them to believe what was written in his name and to trust him."

Sharon:

"Zepherus, how will I be able to speak about all that I see?"

Zepherus:

"Just look around you your mind will remember what it sees. You need not know everything regarding each level you will only be given a glimpse to carry back with you there would not be enough time in your life time to be able to describe what is to be seen in heavens levels."

Sharon:

"As I look to the left of where we are standing I see a large throne I cannot see the face of the one sitting in it though I am only aware of a figure. I see a white garment and a white staff and the voice I hear sounds like billowing thunder with a faint sound of laughter. I do believe that the one seated beside the one I believed to be God was Jesus. Beside the throne in each direction are many chairs and in each of the chairs someone is sitting. They are set up in a crescent formation on each side of the throne. I see many beasts as they wander about and lay throughout God kingdom lions, tigers, panthers they sit at the feet of the holy as a kitten would sit at my feet on earth. The view from the top of the mountain is breath taking the sky is a bright salmon and blue and whispy white clouds float throughout the sky. Just in front of the chairs and thrown to the right of me on the mountain there is a great plain and seated on the ground of this plain as far as my eyes could see were the holy ones of God. Those held in his highest esteem. As I looked to these men I could only think of the shepherds in the bible as they tended their sheep and stopped to rest at a watering hole some carried staffs some carried pouches made of straw. The angels also walked and mingled with the holy. There was singing and music to be heard throughout heaven. In the distance I could see the paths that led to the temple from there I could hear prayer and worship.

I do not know how I am expected to bring any source of justice to what I have just seen. How do I express what a salmon color sky with aqua blue intertwined looks like or a misty green planet in the far away distance in the sky, bright red flowers and fruit trees that grow along the path with every type of fruit imaginable there for your picking anytime you hunger and crystal clear pools of cool water when you thirst? An eternity spent with God sitting before you. Who could ever ask for more?"

Zepherus:

"I believe we have seen enough to carry back to earth with you Sharon. Take my arm and we will leave the first part of this level and descend to the second half of this level they are the blessed."

CHAPTER FOUR LEVEL 1

Part B
The Blessed

Sharon:

"I did as Zephyrus asked and in the blink of an eye we were standing at the doorway to the second part of this level."

Zepherus:

"This is the second part of level one it is also for those closest to God they too have dedicated their lives to him but they did not believe what God himself told them and that is the only way to enter the first level part of this level and sit beside him in heaven for eternity. These too are the holy ones. God loves these souls and knows of their sacrifice, dedication and love for him but his law is the law as written in heaven and what has been written cannot be changed."

Sharon:

"As I look in front of me I find so much peace and beauty. We are in the midst of a mountain range deep in a jungle. There are huge over grown plants their flowers are the deepest of colors they are so beautiful red, orange, yellow, violet, blue, the colors mix together in an array of brilliance. The giant leaves fan out amongst the rocks and waterfalls. Clouds and mist fill the air and the fragrance from the flowers, delight your senses. I can see the holy ones as they enter their temple for worship. These men and women are all wearing a sari form of garment and they all appear to be wearing sandals. Animals are free to roam where ever they want monkeys sit on the backs of the holy ones and play in the trees with the parrots, toucans and myna birds. There are fruit trees scattered about and underneath each tree are benches that encircle the tree. Here the holy ones sit and talk as they eat the fruit and enjoy the conversation they are having. Others wade in the cool water of the spring by the waterfalls.

I can hear the faint sound of a church bell and at that moment I watched as everyone stopped what they were doing and headed towards a path that led up a mountain. I could not see beyond the curve of the path to where everyone was going. So, I asked Zepherus where the path led to and why everyone was going up it."

Zepherus:

"Here the blessed may visit with God when he takes his walk down the side of the mountain. There he will sit by the pool of water and speak of many things then he will give them his blessing before he returns to the top of the mountain."

Sharon:

"Thank you Zepherus you have given me a clearer picture in my mind and this is what I will take back to earth with me."

Zepherus:

"Our time here is over it is time to go on to level two. Take my arm so we may depart."

Sharon:

I held on to Zephyrus's arm and when I opened my eyes we were at the second level.

CHAPTER FIVE LEVEL 2

The Spiritual

Zepherus:

"Sharon this level is for those who have loved God and lived by his laws they worked hard went to church raised their children if they had any, to respect God, the church, the law and the elders. They were by no means always perfect, but once the lord entered their lives they did not waver they were strong against the evils of the world and kept their faith in him no matter what adversity they may have encountered in their life. They understood tragedy to be that of an earthly nature not of Gods doing. When in a situation that they had no control over they did not blame God they merely prayed and asked for his help and guidance. They knew whatever the outcome God would intercede the way he saw fit. Many times the outcome of a circumstance is not the outcome they wanted but they trusted God all the same. This is why they have entered this level. Their reward for their love, spirit and faith in the Lord God is who this, the second level in heaven was created for."

Sharon:

"As we enter this level I find myself listening to the roar of the ocean I can smell the salty air, the light is blinding to my eyes but I can feel the suns warmth on my face as I begin to focus it is exactly as my mind had pictured it to be. I could see the ocean and the sand as it glistened there were trees and flowers and grassy knoll. As I looked around I noticed that we weren't very far from the foot of the mountains. Here the children played at the ocean shore and the men gathered fish in their nets the women looked as though they were preparing bread. They seemed to live in some type of adobe the walls were open and airy. The women wore light cream color robes with a brown rope for a belt the men wore a slightly darker color robe but their belts were also brown. They sat at tables and talked and laughed they were truly full of joy and love. There too, was a multitude of birds and animals. I watched as the young ones climbed the trees for bananas and coconuts, they made a game out of collecting the fruit and they were having fun they truly enjoyed what they were doing. As I looked beyond the huts I could see a temple the songs that could be heard sounded like angels singing. I could see straw baskets being filled with bread and fruit once filled they were placed on the backs of horses and camels. Fish that had been left to dry in the sun were placed in straw mats, rolled up and placed into smaller baskets. Cheese made from the milk of goats were also wrapped in straw mats and placed in baskets. All of these items were also placed on the backs of the horses to carry. The women were gathering flowers the young ones brought the fruit they had been collecting once everything had been packed and ready everyone began to walk to the path that led up the side of the mountain." "Zepherus, can you tell me where everyone is going?" "I asked."

Zepherus:

"Come we will follow behind them and you will see what awaits them at the end of their journey."

Sharon:

"So when everyone had left to go up the path Zepherus and I followed behind them. I actually thought that I would be exerted trying to climb this mountain but I never once tired it was as though the angels themselves had carried me. I actually felt exhilarated once we reached our destination.

I was amazed to find ourselves back on the first level. We watched from the edge of the path there on the plain everyone had gathered, men, women the young the old and the children they all walked and talked among the blessed the holy and the angels. Once again I could see the throne of the lord but I could see only the figure of the one sitting there. The children ran to sit at his feet and they were in awe as they listened to his stories." "Zepherus, what is this? It is wonderful to see everyone together and having such a great time."

Zepherus:

"This is what you on earth call a festival. The first two levels join in a celebration they gather here at the mountain with God and his angles, the holy the blessed and the spiritual. They all eat fruit, bread, fish and cheese they drink wine from cups made from the shells of pineapples and coconuts."

Sharon:

"The chorus of the angles could be heard throughout the mountain as they sang and played their music.

I could hear the stories being told about their lives on earth it was truly amazing to hear the tales being told from the beginning of time on earth until the present. There are sermons to be heard throughout different groups that have assembled on the plain everyone listened to everyone else's story as they ate, drank and laughed.

The festival went on for what seemed to be days to me. The children rode horses played in the waterfalls and swam in the pools. When evening came prayer and worship to the lord could be heard throughout the night, prayers were offered up to God for relatives, peace, guidance and love for those on earth. Some rested nestled among the animals others lay beside each other on straw mats.

There was no discomfort here it didn't matter how much work you did or how much you traveled no one ever seemed to tire. There was no extreme heat in the day and no excessive cold in the night. When morning came the sound of the animals waking up is what you first heard. The roar of the lions, the monkeys in the trees the bird's splendor as they sing their songs for all to hear. I looked to the thrown and saw that no one was there but as I looked to the waterfalls I saw the holy ones as they follow the path to their chairs. The last one to enter was the one to sit upon the throne I still was not able to see more than a figure of a man with his silver staff. After he entered and was seated the rest of the holy also sat. They greeted each other with love and joy and as they looked out among the plain to those gathered there they smiled and waved and nodded their head in greetings to all. Then the most spectacular moment of my life occurred, the one sitting on the throne rose up I could this large figure of a man with flowing hair and beard his garment was a white sash with silver woven throughout the top the bottom was a long cloth that wrapped around his body and I could see a silver spun waist band. He lifted his silver staff to the sky and at that time I could the angels that were carved into it he then held it outwardly over the plain, I could literally see blue lightning bolts as they sparked out from the staff, he bowed his head and in his voice of thunder he spoke for all to hear. I could not understand what he said nor could I see his face but I knew I was standing before God in all his glory."

"Zepherus, I know that I have stood before God yet I cannot see his face and I cannot hear his words all I can hear is the sound of thunder."

Zepherus:

"Yes Sharon, you are still a mortal human and no mortal can set their eyes on the face of God or hear his words this blessing he has just bestowed is for those that have earned the right through death and rebirth into the kingdom of heaven to be with him and his angles. It is only because you are the messenger that you are able to see this. To bring the truth is to see a glimpse into all of heaven.

I believe it is now time to leave this level and go on to the next level. We have seen enough here. Take my arm so we may take our leave and go on to level three."

Chapter Six Level 3

The Children

Sharon:

"I did as Zepherus asked of me and again in a moment time we were at another level.

As I began to focus I could see that we were at the third level, the smell of nature filled the air, I could see trees and meadows full of flowers and butterflies I could hear the sound of children's giggles and laughter. I could hear songs being sung. Out of the corner of my eye I caught a glimpse of a pony as it galloped past us in the woods, its hoofs sounded like crustal wind chimes as they touched the ground. The wind blew softly and the leaves danced in its arms. I could hear the faint sound of a babies coo in the far distance."

Zepherus:

"This is one of my favorite levels it is the level of the children.

We have had to make so many changes on this level recently with so many of the young dying in so many ways there had to be an addition and adjustments made at this level. Here we will visit Tassari and some of the children.

This is a very emotional level for both the children here and for their loved ones on earth. I believe that you must see and absorb as much as you possibly can on this level to bring back to earth with you. There is much to be remembered here."

Sharon:

"Zepherus held my hand and gave it a pat in a gesture on concern when I looked in to his eyes they reassured me of his faith in me.

Zepherus and I walked into the forest in the direction of the sounds we heard. Once we entered the clearing I saw many children sitting in a circle and they all seemed enthralled while they listened to what was being told to them. A woman that had been sitting with a circle of children stood up and began to walk our way. She first stopped and had one of the older children take her place in the circle. As she approached us I recognized her as the angel Tassari from conference. Tassari still wore a rose color robe with a soft pink belt her silver hair looked beautiful in the sunlight and her deep blue eyes gleamed. I couldn't help but notice that the others that sat with the children also had silver colored hair.

Tassari greeted us with her hand held out in friendship."

Tassari:

"Welcome my friends it is truly wonderful to see you this day I have been looking forward to your visit there is so much new to show you since our meeting at conference and we have had many new accomplishments that we are very proud of. Walk with me please, the children will be so happy to have visitors"

Zepherus:

"Thank you Tassari, it is wonderful to see you again also. I have been looking forward to our visit I just finished telling Sharon that this is my favorite level. Not only am I happy to see you again I love seeing the children, they are always a joy to my heart."

Tassari:

"Zepherus it seems like it's been such a long time since conference I have been expecting you and Sharon, there is so much to show you. We haven't quite perfected it yet but with the help from the elders we have found a way to let our children visit with their parents after they have crossed over. We now bring them directly to this level where the other children greet them at this time they are told by the other children that they will be allowed to go back to see mom and dad. When this child goes home for their visit they will be accompanied by another child along with an elder. It seems to be working out better this way I think the smiling face of the children and their capacity to understand the pain these new arrivals are feeling help them tremendously. I saw the fear on the faces of the little ones when they entered the grading area and there was no reason for these children to have to suffer so much fear by having to go to grading when we know that they will be coming here anyway. We haven't accomplished everything that we would like to have accomplished but it is a step in the right direction, I don't believe that we will ever be able to stop all of their anguish they are so young and innocent but we will keep trying to make it as easy as possible for them."

Zepherus:

"I truly understand your plight, I think that it is commendable that you have worked so hard and accomplished what you have up to now. I know how important these children are and have always been to you. You, Tassari are definitely the exception to our rule here in heaven and it is an honor to have you as a dear and faithful friend."

Tassari:

"This Zepherus is not something that came naturally to me as a beta, I have worked with the children for a very long time both here and on earth and I have learned much from both the children and the elders. Look there, Sharon, and you will see the elders as they teach the lessons to the children."

Sharon:

"As we walked we encountered a large circle of children there were both men and women teaching them. As I looked around I saw many elders they talked to the children and held them close. I noticed Tassari watching me with a look of concern on her face."

Tassari:

"Sharon, the elders are the ones who care for the children they are here to greet them as they enter this level they comfort them and wipe away their tears they hold them close and love them. They reassure them that everything will be all right. It is the elders that determine when and with whom the child should go back to visit. It is very mysterious to me as to why some of the children that have passed would want to go back and visit with the parent that has caused their passing. We have many children here that have passed because of the hand of their parent or care giver. This is definitely a human emotion that I cannot comprehend. The elders on the other hand, were humans that have passed and they do understand these human emotions. I have a very difficult time understanding these ways my way would be to help the child not their assailant."

Sharon:"As we talked we were approached by another woman, she too wore a rose color robe with a pink rope as a belt she was a much younger woman then any of the elders were. She had auburn hair and pale green eyes she had a beautiful face and a most trusting smile.

Tassari turned and greeted the woman I could see that she was one of heavens angels."

Tassari:

"Nataria, this is the messenger Sharon go with Zeptherus and Sharon when you return to your level. Zepherus you remember Nataria she is the one that worked so closely with Jacodia on the teen levels. She has brought some of the A level teens here today to teach the children in play. It is always fun for them when the teenagers come to visit. They ride horses, swim with them in the creek and chase frogs on the waters bank. They teach them games of football and baseball. The elders teach them lessons that consist of language, social behavior, and history both on earth and in heaven they learn Gods love of all things and of all the worlds he has created they learn about the stars and the planets of all the galaxies they will visit another section of heaven where creatures from other planets reside. The elders cradle the babies in their arms and they understand the language of babbles and coos they make. The babies in return understand the language of the elders."

Sharon:

"Tassari, do the children ever grow any older here in heaven?" "I see so many little ones." Tassari looked me and smiled.

Tassari:

"The babies grow at a much quicker rate then the older children do, until they reach about four or five, then the rate slows down considerably. We like the little ones to be able to keep up with the other children so they can run and play. It gives them their own sense of independence. And with so many young ones coming in, it would make it that much harder on the elders. So it is the teens that take the children on their travels. And they get the chance to see many things. On their travels they ride the elephants, lay down with the lions, hug the bears, romp with the monkeys, pet the hippopotamus, and eat with the alligators. They sleep in the jungles. Ride camels in the desert, and they swim in the deep blue oceans with the dolphins, whales, shark and fish. They bring fun into these children's existence here to heaven."

Sharon:

"As we walked a little further, I heard the singing from the children. They were holding hands and skipping as they sang their song;

My God, My God, you've given me this day, a day to laugh and a day to play,

A day to sing and a day to pray,

I give you my heart I give you my love,
I thank you for all that you send from above.
I couldn't help tell Tasari how beautiful I thought the children sounded."

Tasari:

"The songs they sing give thanks to our Lord God. They love Him so much and they cannot wait to go to the festival to be near Him. They sit by Him and linger on every word and every sound, just as they would have sat by their earthly father's side."

Sharon:

"As we approached the children in the circle, I noticed that the children all wore white robes but their belts were different colors, and I expressed my curiosity."

Tasari:

"The reason the children have different color belts is to identify the children by entry date. Lessons are scheduled by a child's entry date. It's like being promoted in school, you can't be expected to know lesson two until you know lesson one."

Zepherus:

"Tasari, it has been wonderful to see you and the children today. The messenger has learned so much, but it is almost time to take our leave. Nataria, would you please go and collect the children, we need to be leaving in a little while. Nataria did as Zepherus asked and went to gather the children to take them back with us. She told Zepherus that it would be only a few minutes and they would be ready to leave."

Tasari:

"Thank you Sharon and Zepherus for this visit. I hope you have learned much to take back with you. I also hope this helps the ones on earth that have little ones here, to have more hope and less fear. I must return to my children now, the evening is upon us."

Sharon:

Tasari returned to her circle of children and Zepherus pointed out the sky as the night faded to a deep soft blue with the silhouette of the moons scattered across the sky. Stars flickered in the distance and planets visible to the eye are seen in a fourth dimension. And, we were lucky enough to catch a glimpse of a comet as it passed by.

Zepherus:

"We will soon descend to the teen agers level. Here we will meet again with Jacodia. She has been working with the committee on improving the teen agers levels. We will see what changes have occurred since we saw her at conference."

Sharon:

"Nataria returned with the children."

Zepherus:

"Nataria, please join us as we descend to level four."

Sharon:

"We held on to each others' hands and in a moment we were on level 4."

CHAPTER SEVEN LEVEL 4

Part A
Teenagers

Nataria:

"Thank you Zepherus, this was much faster than taking the long way down here. I don't mind the traveling in the evening but when the children are with me I like to get them back before their lessons begin. It will be dawn soon and I would like to rest for a little while. I believe Jacodia will be bringing new graduates from level B and we need to prepare for their arrival."

Sharon:

"As I looked around I saw meadows and fields where horses ran free. Just beyond the ridge where we were standing. I could see water. I could not distinguish what type of body of water it was, but I could see water itself."

Zepherus:

"I worked with the level A teens with Jacodia when times were different on earth. There wasn't the crime committed by teenagers like there is today. So, level A had many children. Now, there aren't as many teenagers that start out on level A. Some of them come from level B. Most of these children on level A passed over because of accidental deaths or illness. They were really good teens that had good judgment, morals and integrity. They knew right from wrong and chose what was right. They had problems at times, but they worked through them. These children all came from different back grounds. Some had to struggle and worked to buy the newest fashions for school others came from wealthy families, but worked hard in school, all the same. But, neither went with the flow when it caused pain or harm to another person. They would protect rather than harm someone. They didn't laugh at jokes made at the expense of someone else's feelings. They avoided the trouble makers and were comfortable being who they were. They did not hide behind someone else for strength. Their strength of character was enough to carry them through. They were easy and calm with life, themselves, and whatever came along. They could see and understand reasoning and purpose in whatever it was they encountered. These teens were unique and special. Most of them began to excel at an early age and they seemed to have a gift of presence. Everyone knew they were there and for those willing to look inside this child a world of excitement was to be found in just knowing and listening to them. God was preparing these children for the duties they were about to perform once they entered heaven, before they had a chance to become cynical of the world around them. After all, these chosen ones will care for the children here in heaven. They will be their teachers and guide them."

Sharon:

"Zepherus, thank you so much for what you have just given. I will remember every word and everyone that I meet here on this level." I looked to the sky as I began to catch a glimpse in the changing colors. There were bands of violets moving across the sky as if they were being painted by an artist. I could see the different shades as they were hidden in each stroke. And through these changes, I could see the sun. It was encircled by three crescent shaped moons that slowly moved around it. It was truly beautiful. Every step of this journey was just as amazing as another. As Zepherus and I looked around, we saw teenagers as they came over the ridge. They wore robes that were tan on top and light brown on the bottom. Their belts were a twist o tan and brown. Their hair was worn long, and the girls wore cloth weaved throughout their hair. They rode the horses bareback and played some kind of game with tree branches and coconut shells. They gathered berries in baskets. There were groups of teens being taught by teachers. Here the teachers were much younger than the elders that taught the little ones on level three. When I turned around, Nataria was walking towards me. She looked bright and refreshed, and her smile made her face glow."

Nataria:

"Zepherus and Sharon, it is good to know that you have not taken your leave of us yet. I would like you to stay for a little longer and see the teens from level B as they enter our level. Marcarious will be sending them here to us. They cannot cross from one level to another unless a Beta escorts them. If you look to the right of us you will see a small clearing in the woods. There the children will arrive. Marcarious is unable to stay at this time. He and Jacodia must also send some children down to level C. Normally, the levels aren't sent at the same time, but there will be a new group of teens coming in from grading on the next mid day and they need to be prepared for them. The teens are now gathering for the new arrivals."

Sharon:

"I could not believe the number of teenagers that had gathered at the entrance way some waved streamers others carried fruit there was dance and music. I also noticed that some of the teens had lined up two by two, I asked Nataria what the meaning of this meant."

Nataria:

"These teens were chosen to teach the new arrivals of the ways of level A. They are not teachers per say they are called guiders. They will be taken to their lessons and they will go on the journeys with the little ones along with their guiders so that they may journey alone with their own group in the future. These teens from level B will no longer tend to the gardens of food as they did on level B. They will meet with the angels in charge and with their teachers, all teachers were once of earth. We find those with knowledge of earths ways are more prepared when dealing with a situation that may arise on an earthly level.

Sharon look to the sky and see the angels as they rise, this is a guidance ritual. The children must be here, yes, the angels are now sounding their horns concert for the new arrivals."

Sharon:

"As the group arrived they seemed to appear out of nowhere. They stepped down from a small step one at a time, there they were met by their guiders. They were all welcomed by the waving of flag and cheers from the "A"s as they laughingly call themselves. Each new arrival was handed a tan and white robe and a rope belt that was neatly placed on top.

It was so much fun watching these children enjoy this time they had together. They were all so great and I was thrilled to know that they were so happy. I hope this knowledge that I bring back to earth with me will help to ease the pain of the grieving parents that have lost a child."

Nataria:

"Zepherus and Sharon, I must take my leave of you once again, it is time to return to level B my help is needed there. I am hoping to see you again upon your arrival. I am hopeful that Jacodia will be able to meet with you at this time."

Sharon:

"Nataria held my hand for a moment then turned and kissed Zepherus on the cheek she then turned and walked away."

Zepherus:

"It is also time for us to take our leave we have spent much valuable time here. Take my arm as we go on to part B."

Level 4 Part B

Sharon:

"When we arrived at this level I noticed that it was much more confined then any of the other levels that I had already visited there were buildings such as those I had encountered on my walk to the transition area. There were classes being held but they were all in door. It looked much like a high school or college campus on earth. The teens that were walking around campus were quiet and orderly. I saw none of the games being played that I had seen on part A there were no horses being ridden I saw no celebrations of any kind. I turned my head to speak to Zepherus when Nataria walked up behind us."

Nataria:

"My friends, I welcome you to part B. Sharon I can see that you have noticed quite a difference between these parts. Keep in mind that these teens must earn the right to go on to part A. This is a ridged section and much needs to be learned here. Level B teens have had a certain amount of problems on earth before they passed but they were considered hopefuls when they went through grading.

Classes in social behavior and family values are critical in these children's success. They are reinforced in the value of Gods' teachings and his expectations. It is because they were so young when they passed over they were given a chance to go on to a higher section of this level.

Many of these children were abused unloved and unwanted they never experienced any sort of nurturing or love as an infant or as a child. They were at first hurt, when they couldn't deal with the hurt any longer they became angry. Anger infects its own self. It grows it grows inside of one self and consumes thought and reason. Its destruction is endless, and it spreads like a virus.

Many of these children suffered fear, they knew what was right or wrong but because they were fearful of being attacked by their peers they into their better judgment and went along with what was wrong. Other times the fearful found safety in numbers they believed," If I walk alone there is no one to protect me if I join a gang and pledge my loyalty no one will hurt me."

Some of the teens we have at this level committed suicide, teenagers that took their own life. When asked during their session with Markarious the evaluator, what their thoughts were before taking their life this is what many of them had to say. "I didn't want to be made fun of at school, I didn't want to be hit or punished because I was not the biggest or the smartest or the best looking or because I couldn't afford to wear the best clothes, have the best haircut or sporting equipment, because I ware braces or have a bad complexion or because I didn't want to play football or baseball, tennis or soccer, I was never good at sports but nobody cared about that, I was just considered a looser. So I seek out others that like myself, are alone and angry from the abuse. Maybe the games we played weren't safe but they took us out of our reality out of our misery, just for a little while at first then the game of death became our reality. We could no longer distinguish between fantasy and reality. So we took our own lives. To prove what, that we weren't afraid to die, that we were stronger because we weren't afraid? And what of my parents the thought was not to hurt anyone the act was not because I was misunderstood or that I didn't love them because I did it was just an escape from who or what I was told I was and what I came to believe I was."

Do we punish these children for an eternity? I think not. These children are shown the destructiveness of their deeds the pain and sorrow that they have inflected on those that loved them and those that knew them.

Many of their teachers wished that the child had talked to them about their problems and had asked for help. They said that they never knew these children were having any trouble with anyone or that they were in so much pain.

The parents knew that their child was having some difficulties but they thought it was just normal teenage problems the child never discussed anything of a serious nature with them.

What Marcarious was looking for from these children was remorse once he found remorse from these children their other lessons could begin and they could look forward to graduating to part A.

The use of drugs the selling of drugs, car theft and petty theft these issues is also dealt with on part B. That's not saying that everyone here goes on to graduate some do not they are sent down to part once this has happened there is no longer any hope for them there is no return this is where their eternity will be spent. Not all of these children care or show any kind of remorse, for these children there is no hope. They just happened to have passed over before they did anything that would have sent them to part C from the beginning. When they went through grading they were on the edge so they were given a chance. For the ones that have worked hard they will receive their honors to move up after graduation and make that final ascension to part A. All of the children go through the same training session before they are allowed to enter part A. It would seem as though these children would work their hardest to keep their freedom, they are shown through the viewer what to expect on both of the other sections but some of them just do not care. It is still their even in heaven the only difference is they cannot lie and manipulate here all is known. Our teens will not have the opportunity to graduate for a long time if they are held back for any reason. The new arrivals will have the opportunity to graduate at the same time as those held behind will.

I guess that it is hard for some humans to let go of their earthly ways even though they are no longer a part of the earth. It is difficult for some of the adults I would assume the children would find it easier to adjust but that is not true sometimes it is harder for them to let go. Children often see things from a different perspective.

Well I must leave you once again the bells that you hear are telling us of the arrival of our new group.

Sharon I hope you are able to carry this section back to earth with you and show the children where their existence for an eternity will be should they pass oven on their tomorrow. God keep you safe once you return to earth."

Sharon:

"Nataria left us for a final time."

Zepherus:

"Sharon it is now time to go on to the last section of this level. Please take my arm."

Sharon:

"I did as Zepherus asked and held on tightly."

Level 4 Part C

When I focused in on where we where I first noticed that Zepherus was standing beside me with his arm on my shoulder he pointed to the sky. The night began to fade and the sky was a flaming array of reds that over shadowed the dawn. I was just now beginning to see where we were and what it looked like around us. We were standing at the edge of a city. I could smell the concrete and tar from where we were you know the smell after a rain on a hot sunny day, kind of a mixture of buildings streets, parks and trash.

I grabbed for Zephyrus's arm as I saw someone appear from the shadows. I heard a woman's voice and I turned to who was there."

Jacodia:

"It is only I Jacodia do not be frightened. I am here to show you why we try so hard to keep the children on the right path and why we try so hard to make them understand that this level is forever. The first thing that I wanted you to see is the dilapidated school playground and the gang of teenagers sitting on the school steps."

Sharon:

"As I turned I saw the teens, they had on raggedy clothes worn out sneakers skull caps and half finger gloves. There was no music and no laughter to be heard. There was graffiti painted all over the walls and the windows of the school were cracked and broken. The basketball hoop in the play ground was rusted and the net was torn and weather beaten. There were no cars, no shops and no adults anywhere to be seen as Zepherus and I walked the only thing we encountered was squalor, rats and cockroaches. And they walked around in the daylight without a care in the world. The park was over grown with weeds and the stanch from the sewers was unbearable."

Jacodia:

79

"We have made a mini replica of where these kids once lived and went to school only without the protection and maintenance from the adults. We have taken away all authority. This is how they wanted to live with no one to tell them where to go or what to do or what not to do. They turned away from their parents their teachers and their churches. They wanted the riches like the kids on the other side of town had. They wanted the cars and the clothes that they could not afford. They wanted better schools and to be able to go to college. They once dreamed of living in a house with a yard and a dog. These teens did not know how to get there. So they turned their hope into hate their dreams into a quick fix by selling drugs, selling drugs led to greed the greed led to power on the streets. Power led to control and keeping control often led to killing. Is this their fault was the despair they lived with something they chose or is this where society has put these children with no hope. Take a good look in your own city neighborhoods. When was the last time you were even in a neighborhood other than your own? Is it fear of the bad guy or do you fear having to face the way others have to live with every other house around them falling apart with drug dealers and hookers, gang members and drunks on every other corner. There are no supermarkets, hardware stores, theaters, drugstores or restaurants other then fast food. There is only the shell of the buildings where these places once were. And who is at fault? Do you we blame the people that have to live in these neighborhoods or do we blame the absentee landlords that only want to collect the rent from these people that live there. Do we say it's their fault that things are so bad that they like living like this or do you look around and notice that these houses are old they are weather beaten the electrical is nearly one hundred years old as is the plumbing and the sewers. The porches are falling down and the roofs leak, yet these people pay their rent so that they have a place for themselves and their children to live. These people moved in because you moved out and you moved out because you didn't want to worry about the expense of the repairs. So you sit back collect the rent and let the property fall apart because you don't live there. You are nice and comfortable in your suburban home making money off of the house you probably inherited free and clear from your parents. Now let's talk about the jobs where do they find work there are no jobs because there are no neighborhood businesses to hire anyone, the steel plants the manufacturing plants, warehouses, automobile companies they are no longer around. They moved to China or Mexico or India but they are no longer here for the people to work in so they can support their families. So take a look around take a good look around at how these kids must live and think about their hope and their despair and don't ask why they hate and why they want more than they could ever have. Look to within yourself and ask what you can do to save the future of these children. How do you give them hope, give them a future so you can prevent what you are about to see. It all adds up to this their behavior, it cannot be excused because they were taught right from wrong and they chose to take the easy way out but it might help the next one that decides to take that wrong turn down that one way street because this is their eternity."

Sharon:

"As we walked Jacodia pointed these things out to me."

Jacodia:

"The corner store where they used to harass the owners and steal from them is now barren and the food that once was eatable is now moldy or full of maggots. The teens cannot walk down the street without looking over their shoulder to see who might be waiting to jump them or kill them.

Food is delivered once a week to the old football stadium that now smells like stale beer and urine. If you do not get your food before someone else does and they take your share you have to wait until the next week or try to get some off of your friends but when food is scarce and you don't have anything to pay for some it's really hard to find a friend.

There, the young girls young girls huddle in the corner stoop their head buried in their arms that are wrapped around their knees crying for their mothers and there the young boys beg for forgiveness but it is too late because of their refusal to be remorseful and to ask for forgiveness when they had the chance it is no longer an option for them. They are here for an eternity. There is much more to this level Sharon but I believe that you have seen enough to being back to earth with you. It was not easy to have to give up on these children. I know that there are many broken hearted parents and grandparents that have done everything in their power to prevent the things that happened to these children. I do not know how to console them I can only pray that this does not happen to them again."

Zepherus:

"Thank you Jacodia, Sharon has seen enough to take home with her I know this is probably one of the hardest levels to have to deal with, the loss of these children for eternity. Sharon it is now time for us to go on to level 5. Please take my arm."

Sharon:

"I would like to thank you also Jacodia, I have learned much from you and I will do everything in my power to tell the people of what I have learned here." Jacodia held my hand in a farewell gesture. I took hold of Zephyrus's arm and we were on our way to level 5."

Zepherus:

"Sharon before we enter these levels I want to warn you of the evil you are about to encounter, these are where the most depraved have been sent, to live in torment, pain and anguish until the time comes when they will be sent to the lake of fire with Satan and his evil ones to burn for 1000, years. The souls on these levels did not listen to what God had written in His book. This is their eternal punishment.

You need not worry about the fires as we pass through the door ways, no harm will come to you just remember, There is nothing that will prevent their eternity we only pray others will take heed as to what you have to tell them about what you are about to witness."

Chapter Eight Level 5

Drug and Alcohol Abuse

Sharon:

"I could not seem to focus as I looked into this dark and dingy room, once I began to focus I wish I hadn't"

Zepherus:

"This level is for those that have spent a life time abusing drugs and alcohol. They have destroyed their lives and the lives of their friends and families. Many of these abusers began as teenagers smoking some marijuana or drinking alcohol. They liked the feeling they got from being high.

Although many teens experienced with some of these things it did not control their lives they either did not like the effects of these drugs and alcohol or realized that this was not something what they wanted in their lives. They watched as the abusers began to get bad grades drop out if school and isolate themselves from all of their friends that didn't do drugs or drink alcohol. The abusers did not work because they could not stay focused long enough or because they could not pass the mandatory drug tests that most jobs require. They stole money from their parents, grandparents, siblings and even from their friend. So they struggled as they watched those around them grow up and become responsible adults with families of their own good jobs and responsibilities. The abusers if they were lucky enough to have parents that allowed them to stay home, had no thought about anyone other than themselves. They came and went without a care and lived off of mom and dad. They associated only with other abusers like themselves. There were many that did not have the safety net of a family that would put up with the stealing, the disruption and the financial cost. They were given a choice change or get out. Well they didn't want to change they liked the lifestyle they were living they liked to party and they liked to get high. After all it was their life and their choice and they believed no one had the right to tell them what to do. They did not care about the pain that they brought to those that loved them nurtured them and protected them from the outside world as they were growing up. To watch the child you love so much destroy their life and you could do nothing but stand by helplessly and pray that they change their ways. You never gave a thought as to the heartache you caused or the people that you hurt. Where do you go when you won't work when you've used up all of your options by going from one family member to another until there is no one left to take advantage of any more, you end up at this place in your life and if you should pass over before you have asked for God's forgiveness, before you show remorse, it will be too late and here is where you will spend your eternity.

Sharon, take a good look around and remember all of what you see, hear and smell. It is vital to bring this back to earth with you."

Sharon:

"I looked around and the room we were in was full of filth, old clothes, broken bottles, torn mattresses, filthy pillows, a torn chair with the stuffing all hanging out, garbage bags and stench. The windows were covered in black paper so no light could get through. The walls were covered in graffiti with bright red neon paint. Pictures of the devil and the fires of hell were that were painted on the walls seemed to come alive.

The ones condemned to this level, walked around in a drug induced state their hair was long and stringy their skin was dirty and covered with open sores. Most of their teeth were missing and what little food that was visible was half eaten and covered with flies. they walked all stooped over like some kind of zombie you would see on the late night movies. Many of them tripped, stumbled and swayed form their drunk, or drug induced state. They talked to the air when no one was there to listen to them. They fought and screamed at each other, nothing making any sense at all to me.

Zepherus stood in the doorway of this boarded up house and led me down the hallway. Every room was the same, room after room all I could see were pipes, needles, filth and smoke, they snorted cocaine smoked crack, injected heroin used pills, pot, and alcohol.

I wanted to leave this place and never come back. I did not want to remember any let all of what I had seen, heard or smelled on this level."

Zepherus:

"Sharon I know this was not something you wanted your senses to experience but the only way for you to bring back the truth is to know the truth first hand.

Take hold of my arm and let us now leave this level and go on to level six."

CHAPTER NINE LEVEL 6

Liars, Manipulators,

Zepherus:

"This level is the home of some of the most vicious people that ever walked on earth they have destroyed people's lives with their lies, manipulations, and accusations. They have manipulated co-workers to get their job by lying to the boss or other co-workers instilling mistrust and dislike. They gossip telling half truths leaving out true facts replacing them with lies. They smile and pretend to be their friend when in fact all they want is to gain trust, and learn secrets. This information will be used at a later date against that trusting, innocent co-worker or so called friend or neighbor. These people are vicious planting false evidence and trying to destroy someone by stealing pages, erasing important information and files from their computer and then taking credit for their work. It doesn't matter who you are or where you work you must always be aware always have a backup plan if you suspect that someone is trying to sabotage your work, always keep double copies of your work for extra protection. Never reveal something unless you don't care if it is repeated or not. Not everyone is as trustworthy as you may think they are. Trust comes from knowing someone for a life time and even then you can't be sure. So always be aware of liars be aware of those that try to draw you into their gossip if they're talking about someone else to you they are probably talking about you to someone else too. "

Sharon:

"As we entered this level it looked to me as though we were in a huge office building. There were men and women standing around in large groups they were running back and forth from one group to another everyone was arguing and fighting and whispering amongst each other. They were all so angry they are all trying to defend themselves against the lies being told about them, their friends and their families. No one trusts anyone. As they go from group to group each one is trying to control the conversation but as soon as a new person joins the group and tells someone that they are being talked about at another table that person must move on and try to defend them self again. The lies and anger never stop they just keep going on and on from group to group. There is never any rest there is never any peace.

Zepherus I am exhausted from watching these people the amount of energy being used here is incredible just unbelievable."

Zepherus:

"I believe we have seen enough of this level. What more can be said? These people have spent an entire lifetime hurting other people they never once cared who it was that they hurt and it was done only for self gain and self satisfaction. This is where they will spend their eternity. Sharon beginning at this next level and at the beginning of each level that follows I will give you an insight into who, they are how they lived and why these souls will spend their eternity on the level they have been assigned.

Remember the way these humans lived and how their own actions have placed them where they will spend their eternity."

"Sharon:

"Zepherus held out his arm for me and as soon as I touched it we were on our way to level 7."

CHAPTER TEN LEVEL 7

Thieves

Sharon:

"When we entered the next level I looked at Zepherus for a moment he then waved his hand and gave me a view of how some of these people lived their lives on earth. I listened closely as he began to speak."

Zepherus:

"These are some of the lives you will view on this level. The first is Raymond born in Kansas, on July 10, 1941. Raymond was raised on a farm by his mother Grace and father Oscar, he was the fifth born of their seven children. His parents were good hard working people they made a good living and gave their children everything they needed. They raised them to go to church on the Sabbath, have a strong faith in the lord, and to have a high regard for the law. But Raymond was always a little anxious he couldn't wait for anything he quit school to go to work, quit work to go into the service. When he got out of the service he took his money and headed for Los Vegas. He couldn't wait to collect all of the winnings that he thought would come his way. Of course that didn't happen so here he was with no money and no job. He went to stay at a men's shelter there he meet David who was also out of money. David was born in Chicago on November 17, 1929. He had a totally different up bringing then Raymond had. David, was a city kid, raised by a single mom in a tough part of the city if he wanted something and his mother couldn't afford it he stole it, to him it was as simple as that. David and Raymond became quick friends Raymond was impressed with the fact that David could con people out of anything he wanted. They would sit around for hours thinking of way to make quick cash of course David had all the answers. They never would consider getting a job and making an honest pay though. So they came up with an easy way to a quick scam and easy money by hustling the ladies and then robbing them and that's just what they did. Raymond being the youngest and better looking of the two would get the woman to take him up to their hotel room once inside he would take an impression of her room key. David could easily make a replica out of the keys impression that Raymond took. After the key was made Raymond would then call the woman up and ask her if she would like to go out for a drink or dinner. As soon as the woman left her room David was right there to grab whatever it was that he wanted. No witnesses no forced entry the woman simply thought she had left the door unlocked when she left the room because David made sure that he left the door unlocked when he left. Raymond was out with her when the robbery took place so of course suspicion never fell on him. They thought of themselves as the mighty twosome. Soon after they began their scam they met Mindy, born in Los Angeles on January 2, 1947.

Mindy was tall blond and quite a beauty. Her mother and father owned one of the most popular restaurants in Los Angeles. She never wanted for a thing in her life, she had the best clothes went to the best schools and always had money in her pocket but she was always board, always looking for excitement. When she was fifteen years old she was caught shoplifting, she was arrested and her name made the papers, she embarrassed her family and herself. She was doing o.k. for a while but as she got older she wanted more, as she called it, fun out of life. So she soon began making trips to Los Vegas there she could do whatever she wanted and not make the local paper.

Raymond and David caught Mindy stealing a wallet out of the jacket pocket of a man, they approached her and told her that they had seen what she had done, they sat had some coffee and conversation and Mindy joined the scam only she went after the men. They were quite the threesome for a while until the police caught on to their scam and set them up. They were caught sent to prison for a while but as soon as they all got out they resumed their former ways in another city. All three died at the hand of a gun man after they thought they had gotten away with extorting thousands of dollars from him.

Zepherus:

"On earth people take what does not belong to them they do not care who it is that they steal from. Most of these people do not work to pay the things they want and although there are times when they do work they steal from work too. It is wrong, it is all wrong. When they do these things they do it in the corners, they hide in the alley ways to hold someone up they walk down the street to steal your wallet or purse they will steal your car your jewelry, they will break into your home and steal your valuables. They will steal your credit cards your identification your money from your bank account, they will steal your livestock, your pets they steal in restaurants. If you have anything of value to them a thief will take it. They will even steal your children nothing is safe from the hands of a thief.

Be aware thief. It matters not how much or how often you steal your destiny is going to be the same. How do you repay the things that you have taken in your lifetime, how do you give the things back to the people the things they have lost? How do you give someone their financial life back once it has been taken away and destroyed? Maybe you went to prison for a while maybe you got caught that one time but how many times before or after that did you get away with what you did without being punished. You may think that you have gotten away with your crimes but here in heaven we know exactly what you have done. Here you cannot hide your crimes. If you do not stop what you are doing and ask for God's forgiveness from your heart your destiny will not change your eternity awaits you here."

Sharon:

"When I let go of Zephyrus's arm and I began to focus I could see that we were in a wooded area I could hear rustling of leaves and twigs crackling as though someone was walking behind us. I was startled when I looked around and caught a glimpse of a man running through the woods with a bundle of what looked like clothing. I quickly turned to Zepherus I was confused and frightened."

Zepherus:

"Sharon, fear not, no matter what you may see on this journey no harm will ever come to you. The ones that have passed have no power here they cannot harm you in any way they can only experience what they live with here on their own level. You are but a hologram to them."

Sharon:

"Zepherus held my hand tightly as he explained all of this to me. I was comforted immediately after hearing this from him. I really didn't have fear of being harmed I knew Zepherus would protect me but I was startled and of course being human made me forget that I had my own angel to protect me.

As we walked along I saw a small clearing it was only a patch of land and I noticed that it was set in a perfect square. The closer we got to the land the clearer I could see that there were items lying around the perimeter. There was another bundle of clothing a chair, a bed, something that resembled a refrigerator, a small table, a cupboard, a lantern and a few other things that I couldn't quite make out exactly what they were. The odd thing was that they were all setting around the perimeter of the square nothing was in the center.

I then saw a man jump out from behind a chair and he started screaming and cursing. That was when I noticed another man as he grabbed something off of the table and run away with it. Then I noticed there was another person at the other side of his land grabbing his pillows, as he ran to the other side ranting and raving a woman reached over and took his food right out of his cupboard. He did not know what to grab or who to chase but by the time it was over the man was lucky to have his bed still on the ground.

My head was swimming from watching all of this confusion. Everyone that took something headed in a different direction. The owner of the patch of land didn't know which way to go.

I looked at Zepherus and asked him why he just didn't have his things in the middle of the room so these people could not grab them."

Zepherus:"

The material things cannot go beyond the magnetic barrier so these things must remain on the perimeter in the open."

Sharon:

"I almost had to laugh if it weren't so justifiable I probably would have.

When the man finally left his land we followed him to another patch of land that looked exactly like his and we watched as he tried to sneak up and take back something that was taken from him but before he got close enough another man came out from behind a tree and began screaming yelling and cursing as he was swinging a tree branch at him but on the other side of his land someone was taking his food and his boots. It never seemed to end, Zepherus and I watched these people from one patch of land to another and nothing ever changed no matter what they did or what had someone else was there to take it from them. They could not rest when they went to their food drop off point they would try to take as much as they could carry with them because they did not know what if anything would be there when they returned. And they had to go for food or they would starve they never knew if someone would take their last piece of food or not and they couldn't leave it in the woods because someone was always watching them."

Zepherus:

"Come Sharon, it is time for us to leave this level and go on to level eight. Take my arm."

Sharon:

"I did as Zepherus asked I was happy to leave this place I couldn't imagine living an eternity like this, Oh my goodness."

CHAPTER ELEVEN LEVEL 8

Road Rage

Zepherus:

"Nancy born May 11, 1976 in Richmond, she was the only child of Steven and Carolyn. Nancy is quick to anger and thinks she can do whatever she wants because her father is a well known lawyer. She has been stopped twice by the police for driving under the influence of alcohol dad got her off on both accounts. She has had tickets for reckless driving and speeding dad paid the fines. Her reckless driving caused the death of a twenty five year old mother. For that infraction she was given probation for a year and a suspended license for a year. Half way through her probation period she took her dads car on a joy ride, spun out of control hit another car and died.

Timothy, born on March 1, 1966 in Orlando son of Kevin and Amanda, Lives in a nice neighborhood with his wife Clare and their two children, he works construction and Clare is a bookkeeper.

Kevin is hot tempered impatient and a little wild, he screams and curses at people while driving has even gotten out of his car and kicked cars of other drivers that have angered him. He chased a car down an ally one night because this man had cut him off, when he got out of his car to approach the other vehicle he was shot dead. "

Level 8

Road rage

Sharon:

"As we arrived at this level I heard sounds familiar to me and I was surprised to hear these sounds in heaven. They were the sounds of car engines, horns, and screeching breaks."

Zepherus:

"This level is those that have committed road rage when they lived on earth. Many of these humans that passed over have killed, crippled, maimed and terrified other humans while driving. They took their anger out on innocent people while behind the wheel of their vehicle they screamed at people and cursed and cut people off, pass at a high rate of speed causing accidents and death. They would get behind that wheel of a car and used it as a weapon, there is no different from taking a gun out and shooting someone or killing them out of rage while driving. Taking a life is still taking a life no matter how it is done and uncontrollable anger is anger all the same. These people know what they are like and they know their temperament if they choose to drive and have rage they are aware of that fact and they still made the choice and drove. They used other people as targets without a thought or care of their life, or their right to live, walk, play with their children go without pain go to work to support themselves their spouse or their children. They didn't think about the family's that would be devastated because of the loss of their spouse, parent or child. They never think about the lives they are about to change forever this also includes their own families their lives will also be ruined because they will have to live with the shame the loss of a spouse and a parent when they go to prison for their crime, and the financial cost of lawyers and law suits will be devastating.

This level is not only exclusive to road rage this is also for anyone that drives while their ability to drive is impaired under any condition due to the influence of alcohol or drugs. If you harm or cause the death of anyone else because you made the choice to put yourself on the road you can look forward to this level for an eternity. Stop, stop, stop, what you are doing before it is to, late and you become your own victim because once you pass over the choice to your eternity is no longer yours. Just like your victims had no choice as to the time you would cross their path."

Sharon:

"As I began to focus I could see a highway, there were many, many lanes and the traffic was moving at a high rate of speed. People were driving by screaming at each other banging into the back of cars they seemed to be on some sort of highway race track. On the one side of the road I could see what looked like a food market to me. On both sides of the highway people were waiting to cross to get to the market or back from the market. I couldn't figure out what the point of this level was until I watched for a few moments more and as soon as a break in the traffic appeared so did all of these people as they all tried to cross to the other side of the road. They came from both sides of the highway. I was not prepared for what I was about to see next. As they began to cross the highway in both directions vehicles came out of nowhere the people tried to run but there was nowhere for them to run to . I saw bodies as they were being flipped into the air some fell on cars others landed on the side of the road where they were run over by oncoming traffic others landed on the ground and were hit by the traffic coming from behind them. There was blood and mangled bodies everywhere. People were screaming and crying out in pain and many others looked as though they were dead. I looked on in horror, no one stopped their vehicle to try to help anyone, those that could still walk never went near anyone that needed help the only thing anyone seemed concerned about was the food that was scattered about the ground and they were gathering that up as fast as they could.

Well I couldn't believe what happened next, all of the vehicles on the road came to a halt. I watched as everyone that stopped got out of their vehicles that is, cars, trucks, vans, motorcycles, if you could drive it, it was there.

Then the most amazing happened, the people that were injured and the ones that I thought were dead stood up rearranged their broken body parts and limped to the parked vehicles on the road they got into the vehicles and began to drive away. The ones that had been driving were now the one standing at the side of the highway waiting to cross. They once again were coming from or going to the grocery store. It was now their time to cross.

I was still puzzled by the food though and I asked Zepherus why everyone was so concerned about the food after all if they didn't get out of their cars to cross the highway everyone would be o.k."

Zepherus:

"Sharon these people do not know that it is not necessary to have food here, but they do not know what is in store for them either their eternity is to live every day over and over again not to an exact but close enough as possible to their crimes on earth. Today they are the victim tomorrow the assailant and the food is very important to them that is why they must stop, it is what they believe sustains them on their long journey. They do not know why they have to do the things they do they only know they have to do them. It isn't easy to understand the reality of heaven. All it would have taken was to make the right choices in life, if they felt they could not do it on their own all they had to do was to ask for Gods help. God won't change what a person is going to do but he can lead him in a direction to help them self, always remember, free will.

Sharon we must move on to our next level Come take my arm and remember all of what you have seen "

CHAPTER TWELVE LEVEL 9

Animal Abuse

Zepherus:

"Gilbert, born December 24, 1950 in Austin Texas he was the first son of John and Yolanda. Gilbert hunts animals for the joy of killing. He always loved to torture little creatures, he would set cats on fire dismember frogs while they were still alive shoot birds just for the fun of watching them flip around and try to get away. When he turned twelve his dad took him hunting with him but he never took him again after he found him with his elbows deep in gopher's blood and smelling the animal's guts.

John, born April 10, 1965 in Greenville he is the third child born to Teddy and Francis. John still lives on the farm that he grew up on after his parents died. He raises pit bull dogs for fighting he trains them with other dogs that do not have the stamina to fight. There is no mercy for any of these animals. He sets up fighting pens brings in the dogs to fight and makes a lot of money, if his dog loses he is no longer any good to him so if he loses he dies it's as simple as that to him. If he isn't shot he's drowned if he isn't drowned he's hung or starved to death. "

Sharon:

"As we entered this level it almost reminded me of the previous level.

I could smell the fresh scent of the woods. As my eyes focused I could see trees and woods and I could hear the sound of animals crying in the darkness. It wasn't quite light out yet but I could see dawn in the distance.

There was a thickness to the air almost like moisture. I could hear the sound of waterfalls but I couldn't quite figure out where it was coming from. It was eerie, here in the woods there were no stars and no moon in the sky. It was just Zepherus and me and the sound of the animals."

Zepherus:

"Sharon, I find this to be one of the saddest of all the levels that we will encounter. Not that the level itself is sad but the reason that it needed to be created is. Man does not stop to think about all of the things that have been created by God so they destroy and kill for no other reason than annoyance or self pleasure.

God gave man rule over the animals because man was made in his image and he was given an intellect which helped him to discover the wheel build an adobe make use of fire, construct a bridge, build a ship an airplane and a rocket that could go to the moon and beyond. They can grow food in the desert, stop the water from flooding cities, cure disease man can transplant a heart from one person to another. He cooks his food and invents things to make his life easier. This is his intellect but intelligence is not for man alone although he sometimes thinks it is. You are born with intellect your intelligence makes you capable to learn knowledge. This is your intelligence. Stop and look into the eyes of the next animal you are about to kick, punch, shoot, and burn or maim put out into the street to fend for themselves, tie to a tree without food or water in the heat of the sun or cold of the winter to die of starvation or thirst. Look into their eyes and say there is no intelligence behind those eyes.

Of course there are animals that do become vicious and man must protect himself from them. Then of course man does have to eat so the lamb must be slaughtered. This is the meaning of rule over the beasts. Every species lives off of another to survive this are the way the food chain works. But no animal will kill just for the thrill of killing. They do not hurt or maim out of just wanting to. They protect what is theirs whether it be their territory their food or their family. Not much different than man. Yet man will destroy and kill animals for the pleasure of the hunt the thrill of the kill.

For all of those involved in a dog fight or a cock fight where these animals are killed and destroyed just for pleasure or profit for those few dollars in winnings. For big game hunters, kill the beast for your own glory kill the gorillas for their body parts, and the elephant for their tusks, the mink and the wolves for their fur, the alligator for his skin. Kill the mustang because they are eating your grass ,the eagle for a trophy and the whales for the sport. You my friend will spend an eternity reaping what you have sown. Do not laugh or jest or shrug off what you have done behind closed doors because we know all of what you do and no, no, no, no, this is not acceptable. There animals also have intelligence they all have the capacity to love and to hurt. A gorilla will love and protect its own just as you would protect your own. She will nestle her babies in her arms, groom them teach them to pick berries for food, discipline them so they learn what is acceptable in their society she will teach them how to protect themselves from danger, she will to protect her young. There are humans who have done less for their own offspring. A mother bear will carry her cubs in her mouth to a safer home if she feels that they are being threatened and she will attack anything that she believes will harm them this includes their own father. The male penguin will carry the mothers egg nestled between his feet and legs for months while the mother travels deep in the ocean to feed and he will go without food for himself until his egg is hatched and the mother has returned from her voyage. How many human fathers are not willing to do as much as to support their own families. Yet man will go on the hunt to destroy these creatures of God, not for food or survival but for sport or money. Cruelty is also an unforgivable act. If an animal is taught with patients, love and knowledge they will do what is asked of them but to beat an animal into submission is setting that animal to turn on you one day and then you are the one responsible for the outcome of that animals future. May the truth be known, your justice for this abuse and cruelty of these animals will be handed out here on this level created only for you.

Remember clearly what you are about to witness."

Sharon:

"As daylight began to break through I noticed the color of the sky was an unusual grey green not the blue that I was so used to seeing and the landscape was a mixture of woods and jungle . I could feel the fear in the pit of my stomach it wasn't fear of something happening to me I knew that Zepherus was at my side but it was a nervous fear as to what I was about to encounter.

Zepherus and I began to follow a trail. It went up a hill then back down again, it went around in a curve and then it went straight for a ways. There was no rhyme or reason as to why this road was so inconsistent I could not figure out why there were so many twists and turns in a road that could have gone in a straight line. As we walked I could not get that feeling out of my stomach I felt as though we were being watched every step of the way. After we had walked for what seemed to be an hour or so we came upon a small brick structure it was round at the top and widened out at the bottom it was about as tall as a man and no wider then a small room. There were a few windows but they were very small just big enough to let a little air in the room. The entrance looked like that of an igloo you would have to crawl in and out of it to enter or leave. As we walked a little further I could see another smaller room that extended from the back of the building I saw no entrance and only a slit for a window. I almost jumped out of my skin when out of nowhere the sound of a siren went off, this was so unexpected but of course look where I am anything can happen here. Zepherus smiled as he looked at me."

Zepherus:

"I should have warned you about that, it was the siren to alert everyone that their supplies were being dropped off at their assigned location. Everyone here has an assigned location to pick up their supplies on a daily basis every day the pickup point is different and they must make it to that point on time or the supplies are taken away until the next day. We will follow some of our subjects from their home to their pickup point. "

Sharon:

"I watched as a man in the house climbed out of the opening. He was carrying a sack and a club made of wood the club looked like a couple of tree branches tied together. He was very cautious as he stood up and started walking down the path looking from his right side to his left side turning around full circle to see what was behind him and in front of him he was all crouched over as he walked. I could hear something in the woods coming up alongside of us. I tried to keep a close look out I had the feeling that we were being stalked. The man took one look in our direction and began to run he dropped his sack and club so he could run faster whatever was behind us was now on top of him growling and snarling. His screams penetrated right through my ear drum. Zepherus and I ran to where the screams were coming from. Once we were there I could see this man's torn and mangled body as it lay in a pool of blood. I looked up as I heard the sound of a mountain lion growling and snarling, he was looking down on us from the top of a tree his ears were back and his tail was wagging side to side, I almost thought that he was going to attack us next but all he did was watch.

I looked at the man once again and I noticed that he was moving. After a few moments he began to struggle to get back on his feet, he grabbed his wounded arm, blood dripping from his head and face and headed back to where he had dropped his sack. He looked to the sky and made the decision to go forward he limped and tumbled but he still went on. We followed him to the location of his food and supplies he collected what was there for him and put it in his sack he then headed back in the direction he came from struggling every step of the way looking from the left to the right looking up and all around we watched him until he was finally out of sight.

Zepherus and I went on until we came across another structure. This was a replica of the first house. We watched again as another man crawled out of the entrance he to, exited with caution but he had no weapon he was covered in branches. If it wasn't for the fact that he was moving and that I saw him come out of his house dressed like that I would have thought that he was a bush. He too moved with caution taking little steps but he did not stay on the path he went his own way through the woods. We hadn't been following him long when I heard the barking of dogs. The barking of big dogs you could hear them getting closer as they were running through the woods. You knew by the sound of their barking that there was more than one dog. Zepherus and I watch as the bush began to run, it stumbled and began to roll down the hill. This time Zepherus and I began to pick up our pace a little more. As we got closer the screams began these were intense blood curdling screams. I didn't even want to go any further but we continued to follow the sounds. When we got there we encountered three huge dogs two Rottweiler's and a pit bull. These dogs were tearing and biting at every part of this man's body they were relentless, the flesh was literally torn off of his legs and arms he had branches still tucked down his pants but other than that there was not a place on his body with some sort of wound. The moans cries were horrific my heart could not stop pounding. The dogs took a long look at Zepherus and me gave us a snarl and turned and walked away. This man got up grabbed his sack from around his waist and hobbled to where his supplies were. He packed his sack and headed for home his whimpering could be heard through the woods as he walked away.

We went on once again to another structure this again was just like the first two. When this man came out he was wrapped all in rags as though he wanted to protect his body from something. He scurried along the side of the road never stopping to look behind or to either side he just went straight ahead. He moved so fast that he made it to his supply drop off area without being caught by anything. He hurried as he put his supplies in his sack and scurried back in the same direction that he came from, I thought that he was safe, I thought that he would make it home without a problem when I heard the sound of hoofs coming toward us. Zepherus grabbed my arm and pulled me back just as this gigantic horse ran past us. It must have been a Clydesdale it was so huge. We watched as the man began to run but in a moments time this horse was on top of the man pounding him with his hoofs over and over again and there was nothing the man could do to protect himself other than try to cover his head with his hands and arms but little good that did by the time the horse was through the man's head was crushed and his leg was turned around in the opposite direction, the bones in his arms were poking through his skin and he was covered with welts and bruises on every inch of his skin The horse looked our way gave us a snort pounded his hoof on the ground and galloped away. This man that I thought would never move again sat molded his head back in shape turned his leg around as he screamed in pain stood up and scurried to pick up his sack with his supplies stuffed them back into the sack and ran back to his house.

The next person that crossed out path was a woman we watched her as she gathered up her food. She wore a long skirt, a sweat shirt with a hood, a wide brim hat and long gloves. She watched with caution as she filled her bag. She looked to the sky with a constant eye toward the trees as she began to leave the sound of a hundred birds came out of nowhere. The birds were upon the woman before she could even take a step away from them. They dove at her they pecked at her they swarmed her no matter which way she tried to turn they were all over her, she fell to the ground and they continued to peck, peck, peck at her arms at her legs at her head, they pulled out her hair, her one eye rolled on the ground her clothing was in shreds and her flesh was full of holes. The birds began to fly away, as quickly as they came then the last bird that was sitting on her back turned and looked our way, gave a squawk and flew away over my head. I could actually feel the breeze from his wings on my head. Again the woman I thought would never get up again was picking herself up off of the ground putting her eyes back in their sockets. She took off the shreds of material from her arm and wrapped it around her head and legs she picked up her sack and headed for home.

I was expecting Zepherus to say that it was time to leave but he didn't so I just followed him to the water falls. Here we sat for a moment then he pointed to a man on the other side of the river that was crossing the river to get to his supplies. He made himself a floating devise out of tree limbs and leaves. This I thought, I would have to see get across the river. He got on the so called raft and pushed himself off but about half way there he began to sink. That is when I saw the ripples in the water, a long tail and a mouthful of teeth. It swam to the man and started tearing at him it took him up and down around and around in the water holding his body in his strong jaws. When he finally decided to let go the man was floating face down in the water and there he stayed until he drifted to shore. He then crawled out of the water repositioned his torn arm back to where it should be stood up and painfully struggled as he went to get his supplies. Now his biggest problem was how to get back to the other side of the river once again. "

Zepherus:

"I know this journey has been long we have but one more step to take on this level. "

Sharon:

"We left the river and walked deep into the jungle when we came across another man leaving his house. He carried a basket with what looked like fruit with him. This I thought must be a long journey if he has to bring his lunch but shortly after he left we watched as he encountered this group of gorillas on his path. The man didn't know which way to turn, he tried to offer them fruit but they began circling him as they jumped up and down screeching and growling and taunting him. If he moved to the right they moved to the right if he moved to the left they moved to the left. The man could not go anywhere or do anything so he sat down on the ground and began to cry. The gorillas taunted him even more and they sounded as though they were mockingly crying back at him. One of the gorillas moved forward and punched him in the head than another moved in and then another they were punching and pulling and biting him they were pulling him and throwing him around as though he was a rag doll. They stomped and jumped and pulled his hair out in clumps there was blood running down his face his arm was pulled out of the socket and left to dangle. When the man couldn't move anymore they stopped and walked away one at a time when the last gorilla was left he stood over the man and looked our way, he beat his chest and shook his head as he screech at me and turned away following the others into the jungle."

Zepherus:

"I know that you have seen much here Sharon but there are many, many more crimes against animals but I believe you have seen enough to carry back with you. I am sure that you noticed how the animals always turned and looked at you as though they knew that you were here for them and they were saying thank you."

Sharon:

"Thank you Zepherus, yes this was a long stop on our journey but from what I have seen of this level it is justice for these poor animals. Yes, I did notice the way the animals said, good- by to me and I could feel their heartfelt gratitude."

Zepherus:

"Come take my hand our journey here is over now we go on to level 10."

CHAPTER THIRTEEN LEVEL 10

Racism

Jeffery born in Augusta on August 4, 1950, son of Billy Joe and May he was raised in the country. Jeffery was taught at an early age to hate, his dad hates, his uncles hate, his cousins hate so of course he is going to learn to hate too.

At the age of six he was playing with a little black child in the parking lot on Sunday after mass when his saw him he dragged him away and when he got him home he switched him so bad he couldn't sit for days. Jeffery learned real fast to stay away from the other black children in town and the words of hate grew in his mind.

Racism

Sharon:

"As we entered this level I could hear nothing but yelling and arguing I couldn't quite make out what was going on but I knew it did not sound friendly. I looked at Zepherus and he just stood there shaking his head."

Zepherus:

"You know Sharon this is one level that I completely do not understand. It makes absolutely no sense to us in heaven as to why humans are so prejudice, why they hate truly hate someone because of the color of their skin, their nationality, their religious beliefs or their sexual preference. They kill in the name of the Lord, this is not what God wants what he wants out of the people is love and peace this is what he teaches but on this level no one ever seemed to understand this. I hope that you can find a way to help the people understand that Gods love is for all people hate will never get anyone into heaven. Watch this level very carefully so those that carry a heavy heart of hate will understand where they will spend their eternity."

Sharon:

"I could see that we were standing in a clearing it looked like we were maybe in the grand- canyon or at least somewhere like that. I could see ridges and mountains behind the clearing and the colors were absolutely beautiful, purples, oranges, yellows all mixed and mingled throughout the mountains, reds, tans, browns and greens weaved themselves in the canyon floor. This was truly a piece of heaven. The sounds I heard were so distracting. I followed Zepherus as he headed in the direction where the noise was coming from. We stood on a ledge and watch those below us. There in this huge clearing people were sectioned off in what looked like sliced pie shaped cubicles. There were clear plastic walls only about waist high but it didn't look as though anyone could cross over them. I must have been able to see at least thirty of these sections. In front of each cubicle a sign was hung. I could not believe what I was reading the first sign I saw read: We are catholic. The next one read: We are white, power to the K.K.K. and the Arian nation: next Black power: next Latino live: next only Jewish allowed: next Chinese above all other nations: next Irish forever: next: Hail to the Queen England tradition: next European solidarity: next Equator freedom: next Divide Africa. The signs went on further than my eyes could see and everyone was calling each other names. They were falling down from heat exhaustion their faces were all twisted and the veins in their necks were ready to pop. Some threw stones some were spitting others shook their fists to the sky. These people were so consumed with their hate they could not see the beauty that surrounded them. Many would not stop screaming and cursing, long enough to get their food and water supplies when they were brought in.

The fire red sky turned pitch black and a thousand stars shined but no one bothered to see the beauty to see what God had created. Their hands were cracked and dry their lips were blistered from the heat of the sun but they continued all the same name calling cursing and threatening one another. They burned flags wore bandanas some wore hoods or masks others painted their faces, all of this in the name of hate.

I looked at Zepherus with a pleading eye to take me away from all of this hate."

Zepherus:

"I know you are ready to leave this place just remember all of the hate that you have seen here at this level and where it will take these people that hate so much. All of these souls are so consumed with their hate that they will never have a chance at happiness. They will never have a chance to love or have a chance to smile. It is a sentence they have written down in their own handwriting.

Now, take my arm and we will go on to level 11"

CHAPTER FOURTEEN LEVEL 11

Selfishness
Greed

Zepherus:

"Spencer was born on October 3, 1940 in Louisville son of Malcolm and Rebecca. He was raised on a thro bred horse ranch and was surrounded in luxury all of his life but he never wanted to share anything he had with anyone. Even as a child he didn't want give his old hand me down clothes to the poor people that live in the community. If he saw a child wearing something of his that his mother had given away he would tell them to give it back. His daddy thought this was cute, good business sense is what he would laughingly tell his wife as she cringed in embarrassment. As Spencer got older he never dated because he didn't want to spend his money on a girl. When his mom died he still lived at home and when he thought his dad was spending his money foolishly he had his dad deemed incompetent and then placed in a home and Spencer remained on the ranch by himself. Three years after his father was put in a home Spencer had a fatal heart attack. The housekeeper found him lying on the bathroom floor when she came to work one morning. Spencer never once in his life tried to help anyone, he had no friends and no surviving relatives, except his father and he was considered incompetent. The state took over the estate and used the money to pay for his father's expenses.

Selfishness

Hank, born on July 4, 1979 in Ottawa mother Noreen father Joseph wife Ellen father of Justin and Mark. Hank was a very successful in business. He drove a nice car had a beautiful home, good looks, great job and anything money could buy. He had nice wife and wonderful boys. What Hank didn't have was generosity not only with his money but also with his love and time he had no generosity of spirit. His wife lived in a beautiful home his boys went to the best of schools but Hank was selfish with what he could give to others of himself. When a birthday came up he was never there at Christmas time Hank would rather be at a football game out of town or on a golf tournament, for the boy's graduation, or plays, or sporting events, Hank was always away on a business trip. He never made it to his own father's funeral he said that he couldn't break his appointment with his out of town client. His wife learned to go her own separate way, the boys learned that dad wouldn't be there too, canceled camping trips, baseball games, soccer and school events. Ellen was a good woman and a loyal and faithful wife throughout the years but after so many disappointments, and heartaches, she one day realized there was no longer any pain in her heart, his obsession with himself and his lack of caring had destroyed the passion she once held in her heart for him. Although her heart still held love it no longer had hope.

On a rainy October night Hank had come home late from a business trip, everyone knew that he was supposed to come home but when he didn't show up on time no one really thought anything about it. This was typical for Hank, no phone call to say he'd be running late or even that he wouldn't be coming home at all so the boys did their studying and went to bed and his wife took her shower and went to bed.

Hank lay outside on the ground in the rain for hours he had a massive heart attack and stroke he could not move or cry out for help. No one looked out the window for Hank no one paced the floors or worried about him no one gave him a second thought as they prepared for bed. By the time the boys left the house in the morning to catch their bus for school it was already too late for Hank because no one bothered to look out the door, he laid there and had hours to think about his life before he died and do you know all he thought about was himself , how would he live through this, how will he be able to go to Cancun next week, not one thought about his wife and children other then where are they, why doesn't someone look out the window and see me. Hanks family mourned as any family would mourn a loved one only they didn't have good memories to miss with this man they only missed what they wanted their lives to be like with this man that gave them nothing."

Sharon:

"The first visit of this level brought us to the home of an elderly man. It was a beautiful, meticulously kept home. The gardens were exquisitely maintained and there was a beautifully designed swimming pool in the swim room in the back of the house. There were three antique cars in the driveway and servants throughout the house. The man of the house sat in his office it was the most gorgeous office I had ever seen, it had Italian inlaid tiles the fire place was the length of the wall and original sculptures and trophy's sat on the mantel. The art work hanging on the walls are also original paintings. He had a collection of first edition books among the books that sat on the shelf of his bookcase, on his desk sat a picture of his yacht, his jet and his summer home. It's funny though I never saw a picture of his wife or children in his office. The only way I even knew that he even had a family was because of the pictures that were on the piano in the living room. I listened as the man spoke to his lawyer on the phone."

Greedy man:

"I don't care how many people have to lose their jobs they're costing this company money, they're costing me a lot of money they can do without health insurance let them pay their own premiums. They can do without any raises, who do these useless, worthless peons think they are anyway? I've built this company from the ground and they're not getting another cent from me. Do you hear me? They will not get another red cent from me or my company. I'll bring my business to China or Mexico or India, anywhere I can go where I'll save some money. Close the plants close them all this is my money. I'm sick of all these loafers all these people that want to sponge off of me, off of my hard earned money."

Sharon:

"As I listened to this man I thought what, what. What about the work these people do for you to earn their money. No wonder this country is in the state it is in. You took the jobs away from these people so that you could live like this, with your big houses, cars, jet and yacht. What about the food they have to buy for their families, or their mortgage and car payments they have to make. Do you not think these people are entitled to live the American dream? All they want to do is a hard honest day work for an honest day pay so that they can give their children a better life.

So close your plants, keep all of your money for yourself and you can sit back and wonder why your sales are down and your profits are down and the products you had manufactured and brought from overseas are falling apart and being recalled. Do you really think that someone thousands of miles away, in another country cares whether or not a wheel falls off or the paint chips have lead in them.

Now, how is the person who lost their job and ran out of unemployment, went on welfare or found a job making minimum wage, if they were lucky enough to find a job, how do you expect these people to buy your products, or do you think they may be forced to buy the cheapest products they can find?" So your greed has made you rich and your children expect everything to be handed to them and your wife sits back and talks about the lower class with her friends and everyone thinks they are better than everyone else. Now, you hoard your money spoil your children and die with your money in the bank. Your greed my friend is why you will spend eternity on level 11.

I took Zephyrus's arm and we went on to our next visit.

This was far from what we had just seen we were outside of an old falling down farmhouse it's windows were cracked, paint was faded and pealing on the house and barn, the fence was falling down and the weeds were over grown. As we entered the house I noticed at least a dozen cats walking around all over the cupboards and tables, they walked on top of everything and the odor was atrocious. There was food rotting on the cupboards and the sink was full of dirty dishes. There sitting in a chair in the parlor was this old woman, her hair was not kept and her clothes were tattered she had cats crawling all over her and around her. This poor thing I thought, where is her family where is someone to take care of her. At that moment there was a knock on the door and she got up and peaked through the curtains she began to mumble to herself."

Old woman:

"Here they are again here to get my money well, their little ploy isn't going to work they aren't getting a cent out of me. They can't make me leave my house they can't make me go anywhere this is my house."

Sharon:

"The knock at the door became louder. It was the old woman's son."

Son:

"Mom, let us in, mom answer the door."

Sharon:

"I heard this man say but the old woman went back and sat down in her chair. Her son walked to the back door and slipped his hand through the crack in the window and got into the house he then went around the front and let his sister in. They looked around the house at the mess and shook their heads."

Son:

"Mom you can no longer live like this you will have to come with us to the home, we found you a very nice place to live and you will be well taken care of there. You refuse to come and live with either of us because of the children and we have no other choice."

Sharon:

"With that they began to pack some of her things but she wasn't going anywhere without a fight she was yelling and screaming at them to stay out of her room. Now this woman never gave her children a thing, they ate day old bread, wore second hand clothes and every extra minute they had was spent helping their dad on the farm until he passed away a few years earlier. She always cried poor, no matter how hard her husband worked, or what he did it just wasn't enough to please her. The woman always took care of the bookkeeping and finances, always crying there wasn't enough. The kids left home and went to work to and paid their own way through collage they married and had their own children and the grandchildren never received so much as a birthday card from her but her children always made sure to send her money every chance they got.

This time they were not kidding or letting her talk them into letting her stay. The winter would soon be here and they were worried that she might freeze to death. They went to court and signed the necessary papers stating that they would pay for her expenses and they were now going to take her out of the shambles that she lived in. They always tried to have work done on the house and on the farm but every time someone came to the farm she refused to allow them on her property and threatened to have them arrested for trespassing.

The old woman sold off all of the cattle, the horses, the farm equipment and parcels of land. Her excuse was that she needed to support herself. Well now there was nothing left to sell and the kids wondered how she would survive.

The sheriff came to the door with the papers they needed and took her out of the mess she was living in. She never stopped cursing them and calling them thieves and ungrateful brats the daughter cried and the son held his head down this was not something either one of them wanted to do. They got her in the car and took her to the assisted living residence where she would be living. She told them to get out and to never come back and to stay out of her house but they had to go back to take care of the animals and find homes for all of the cats. While they were there they decided to clean up as much as possible. When they went through the mother's room they noticed a few loose boards on the floor when they picked up the carpet and removed the loose boards they almost had a heart attack, there stuffed deep into the floor were stacks and stacks of money, they started pulling out all of these hundred dollar bills, checks that had never been cashed worth thousands of dollars. They could not believe what they were seeing. Here this greedy old woman that couldn't even give her children fresh bread and fruit and kept her husband working like a dog until the day he died had been stashing this money away for years, they even found life insurance policies that were left to them after their father died and a policy left to the mother in the amount of five hundred thousand dollars and here they pooled their money together to pay for their dads funeral, which never mattered to them they loved their mother and father and did not mind helping out.

Well the total amount stuffed under the floor boards in cash, checks and insurance policies was more than five million dollars. When they went to question their mother about the money all she kept saying was. "

Old woman:

"Mine it's all mine I did without all these years so I could have it all and when I get out of here I'm going away so no one can take my money it's mine all mine, I worked all these years saving it. You took my life away from me when you were born I was supposed to be a star and now it's my time and my money. I can go anywhere in the world that I want without you two holding me back."

Sharon:

"They just looked at each other and shook their heads. They always knew that their mother had resented them for holding her back from going to the big city and becoming famous but they never knew that it had become such an obsession with her.

They left their mother sitting in her room ranting and raving about her money and they went home. They sold the farm and soon after that, the old woman died of a heart attack after she had a fit about her money. The kids finally got to enjoy what their mother had kept them all their life."

I took Zephyrus's arm and we were in a room with hundreds of people. There were tables filled with everything imaginable, clothes, tools, toys shoes garden supplies, furniture, makeup cosmetics, personal items, groceries, appliances, you name it and it was there. And the hundreds of people were grabbing and fighting and yelling all I heard was, that's mine give that to me, don't touch that, keep your hands off, mine , mine, mine everyone was pulling and grabbing and pushing and shoving, they were stepping on each other's feet and pushing people to the ground. They were crying and laughing running and jumping all over the place, no one stood still for a moment. Zepherus and I worked our way from the madness and to another section of this level I couldn't believe what I saw, it was a banquet with every kind of food imaginable I looked over the table and everyone was stuffing their face with food and I mean stuffing, they had mouthfuls of roast beef, fried chicken, pork chops, lobster, shrimp, grilled fish, meat loaf, spaghetti, goulash, stews, soups, mashed potatoes, fried potatoes, scalloped potatoes, baked potatoes plain and with cheese and butter and sour cream, there were French fries, curly q fries and home fries. There were bowls filled with gravies and cream sauces, rice, pasta, there were tons of salad, fresh lettuce, potato salad, macaroni and crab, I saw Chinese sweet and sour, hot and spicy, shrimp, chicken and beef stir fry, there was Italian lasagna, sauce with meat, sauce plain, sauce with meatballs, eggplant parmesan and sausage. The more I looked the more I saw, corn on the cob, cream corn, green beans, pork and beans, asparagus, beets, cucumbers, radishes, tomatoes, peppers and onions fresh and fried. Then the deserts, cake with icing cake with sauces, butter rum, orange cream, spice nut with caramel sauce, chocolate fudge, chocolate brownies, chocolate chip cookies, peanut butter cookies, raspberry tarts, cherry turnovers, cheese Danish, ice cream, donuts. I could go on forever it was a feast and no one stopped eating, they just ate and ate and ate, and when all the food was gone there were people laying on the floor grabbing their stomachs in pain, they rolled around moaning and groaning in pain they were passing gas, some were throwing up all over themselves, they were running to relieve themselves. I looked away in disgust and when turned back I could see the people at the tables in the other section they were still grabbing, pushing and screaming at each other. I looked at Zepherus"

Zepherus:

"Sharon, you look as though you have had enough of this level ,take my arm and we shall leave. Remember all the greed and selfishness you have seen here on this level. Many of these people do not think about what they are doing, they do not see beyond their own greed, I only hope that you can make them see what they are doing. I don't know what more I can say to you regarding these people or this level. Come Sharon take my arm and we will go on to our next level."

Sharon:

"I did as Zepherus asked of me and we were on our way to level 12."

CHAPTER FIFTEEN LEVEL 12

Harassment

Zepherus:

"Ronald, born in Jamestown on June 11, 1956 son of James and Karen, second of five children. Always had a problem with getting along with other people even as a child he would torment his sibling, break their toys hit them and push them down, he could not get along with anyone in school and tried to control those that could not defend themselves If he was angry at someone for any particular reason he would follow them around, knowing there was nothing anyone could do about it. No law in following someone that's how the law looked at it. Other times he would verbally make comments to someone knowing that the person would physically do him harm then he would have that person arrested and later sue them for all kinds of damages. If Ronald thought a girl should return his advances toward her and she didn't he would follow her everywhere, home from school, to the mall, to sporting events, he did not leave her alone he would call her names and make sexual gestures at her he was relentless. Even the problem kids at school wanted nothing to do with him. As he grew to an adult his behavior never changed it just progressed, and the harassment went on to people at work, neighbors anyone he came in contact was at his mercy. He had court case after court case against him, he would get an order to stay away from these people but the minute the order was up he'd start all over again, this went from neighbor to neighbor and township to township. He once bragged that he had been arrested over fifty times and never spent more than a night in jail and there was nothing anyone could do to stop him because he knew his rights. This finally came to an end one evening when he followed a man from work home that he had been stalking and harassed every day. The man tried to confront him but he would always hide but this one evening when he was following this man home to see where he lived the man got out of his car and took a gun out of his jacket and shot him in the head. They found Ronald's body in his car in a pool of blood, but because he had so many enemies the authorities never found his assailant.

Take a good look around you it shouldn't take you long before you grasp who this level involves. You know Sharon it has never ceased to amaze me as to what the humans are capable of doing to each other."

Sharon:

"As I looked around me I could see what looked like a neighborhood only the houses were inches apart and about ten feet high and ten feet wide."

Zepherus:

"Walk closely by my side, I want you to see as much as possible as we walk through this level. It isn't a very long journey but there is much to be seen here. The evilness that these people have inflicted on other people is incomprehensible. "

Sharon:

"The first thing that I saw was a man standing on his porch with shreds of paper in a bag he was throwing them all over the lawn of the person next door to him, then he ran inside his house and peaked out the window and watched as the neighbor came out of his house yelling. The man stood in his doorway laughing and rubbing his hands together in joy, he loved the torment he was doing.

The neighbor next door in retaliation set his speakers out on his porch and began to play the music. It was so loud so loud it was vibrating the windows next door. This man then ran into his house and peaked out his window as the neighbors on both side ran out of their houses screaming and yelling and cursing. We continued to walk and at the very next house there were garbage cans with the lids wide open the smell was bad enough but the maggots falling to the ground and crawling under the house next door was worse. The next encounter was a man hiding on his porch and he had his penis out and he was waving it at the woman across the street. The woman's husband came running after the man but he darted into his house closed the door and stood there laughing at the man. As we passed by the next house we heard the sound of a car alarm and horn beeping it was deafening to my ears. The house next door was even louder someone in there was banging and pounding on the walls, a dog tied in the back yard never stopped barking. We watched as the neighbor next to that was pulling parts of his neighbor's house off and bringing it in side of his own house, he then walked over and began nailing his gate to that neighbors house. Next to him the neighbor was spraying his next door neighbor's freshly planted flowers with weed killer. At the next house the man was draining his pool into his neighbor's yard, causing it to flood, and kill the rose bushes that were planted there. In the very next yard I watched as a man jumped over the fence and slashed his neighbor's pool. The next house the man stood outside cursing and saying things in an abusive manner about the people that lived next door to him. He was making filthy sexual comments like, come and swim in my pool my d.n.a. is running down my leg. At the next house the people were shooting fireworks at the house across the street and setting them off at any time day or night. Next door to that someone is blasting music about the devil, how appropriate. At the next house we come across there is a man standing in his driveway throwing eggs at the car next door to him. The next house had sings hanging all over his house and on his front lawn with arrows pointing up and down the street with insulting comments about the neighbors written on them while all the time he has one in his front window claiming to be an advocate of peace, what a misconception this man is. The next neighbor is throwing trash in the street in front of the house next door, jugs, pieces of torn up cardboard, dirty paper towels, snack bags, paper cups, dirty diapers. I don't understand how someone could enjoy being so nasty to other people. The next person we encounter is throwing his dogs feces onto his neighbor's lawn. The person next to them was yelling racial comments to the people that lived down the street because they were a bi-racial family. It just keeps going on and on it never stops and then they lie about what they're doing and try to blame someone else.

Zepherus you are so correct in saying that it wouldn't take long for me to recognize this level as a level about harassment, I too have encountered all of these forms of harassments myself from a neighbor my so I can fully understand the necessity of such a level being here, no one should have to endure such behavior from anyone, it is good to know that justice will be served in eternity for these cruel and hateful people."

Zepherus:

"Sharon people lie and think they are getting away with things on earth and maybe they will fool the police and the judges or maybe it's not something that is important to anyone other than the people going through this torment but for the suffering that these people have had to endure they will find their justification in heaven.

Take my arm so that we may leave this level."

Sharon:

"I did as Zepherus asked and we went on to level 13."

CHAPTER SIXTEEN LEVEL 13

Environmental Abuse

Zepherus

"Fredrick was born April 16.1949 in Salt Lake City. He is the only son of Aaron and Julia. Fredrick was an executive for a major Chemical company. Fredrick always liked to make money and he was good at his job they paid him well and he was well respected but Aaron lost his integrity somewhere down the road. He hid research reports on the dangers of dumping the chemicals into a landfill. He sabotaged his co-workers reports to hide the truth regarding the devastation that some of these chemicals would have on human and animal life if they were not contained properly and when it was brought to his attention that some of the projects that he had given the ok on before the final reports had come in were a dangerous mistake he changed them to try and cover up his mistakes but then the bottom fell out, the chemicals were leaking out of the barrels that they had been buried in and now this was a major problem because they had been buried all across the country and were now leaking hazardous waste into the fresh water supply system lakes ,ponds, wells and farmland were all being contaminated causing deformed birds and wild life. The physical deformations and death related to these spills were too many to tally the mutations the birds and the animals suffered are yet to be documented.

Fredrick was found responsible and judged guilty of his actions and sent to prison there he died of lung cancer two months after being sentence.

Sandra born May 15, 1973 in Seattle, father Greg (deceased) mother Diane. Sandra inherited her father's lumber company after his death she always went on field excursions with her dad and she watched for years as the environmentalists fought her father regarding the destruction of the forests in the north western region of America and in the rain forests of South America. Her father never cared and he never lost a court case that was brought against him, he would laugh as he defended himself by saying "People want wood Sandra they need it if they didn't I wouldn't be able to sell it, don't ever let these bleeding hearts get in your way." And she didn't she listened to every word she had been raised with, she became just like her dad cutting down thousands of trees that were an important part of the rain forest in Brazil displacing people and animals, birds, snakes and bats all of God's trees and creatures that are detrimental in keeping the balance of nature. For every tree, bird, snake and bat that are destroyed the insects double and triple destroying many plants that can only be found in this region. Many of these plants were being used for medical purposes. The crops were also being destroyed because insects were no longer controlled by the birds, bats and snakes that fed on them.

One day while Sandra was on a field excursion a tree limb fell from a tree hit her on the head and killed her.

Sharon, take my arm as we begin our journey on this level, it is not a very long journey but if man does not change this is all that will be left of your earth and this is the sentence that man him placed upon himself."

Sharon:

"I did as Zepherus asked and took his arm I remember the feeling of fear in the pit of my stomach as I held on tightly on to his arm."

Environmental Abuse

Sharon:

"When I had completely focused I wasn't quite sure what I was looking at, I saw a lake and some dead trees, there were dead animals and birds lying on the ground these animals looked really strange though, some had missing limbs, extra eyes, deformed beaks and wings, I saw animals with larger than normal heads others with smaller than normal heads, I saw rodents the size of dogs with teeth that looked as though they could bite your arm of with one quick nip. I noticed that there were ducks with claws and birds with duck bills, there were animals struggling to walk on deformed limbs or limbs that were too small to carry their body weight, animals struggling to eat because their mouth's were so crooked they could not maneuver it properly to get the food in their mouth.

As we approached the lake I noticed it was all sludge and the creatures that were swimming around in it were anything but fish, they had a lizard type of skin and their eyes were small and blinked to the side they had gills but they were on the top of their head and extra wide with a fleshy screen that looked as though it would be used as a filter and they had webbed feet with claws. This was all terrifying for me to see. There was no grass only tumbleweed blowing around the sky was a frightening glowing orange red.

We walked to the other side of the lake there I saw what was similar to a camp ground. The heat was unbearable and the stench from the lake was turning my stomach as we approached the camp and I saw the people I noticed that they were filthy from the sludge they had boils and open sores on their bodies their clothes were torn and dirty and their hair was matted and falling out, many of them looked as though they had missing or no teeth at all. A strange thing I noticed was that the clothes they had on looked as though they were really expensive at one time the men had on suites and the women had on skirts and blazers, their shoes were probably the finest leather because although they were filthy and worn they held up good in this mess that they in. There really wasn't much more to see as Zepherus and I went from camp to camp, it was all the same deformed or dead animals humans living in waste and decay. I really can't add any more to this level the environment is what it has become through neglect and greed, chemical contamination and the destruction of the ozone.

I remember thinking," this is not the way anyone would want to spend their eternity, with all this hopelessness." I turned to Zepherus with a look of sadness."

Zepherus:

"Sharon there isn't much more to see on this level all of the damage has already been done. There is no hope here, just like the damage they have caused on earth there is no bringing back that which is already dead.

Take my arm and I will take you out of all of this waste."

Sharon:

"Thank you Zepherus this is so sad all of this for what the price of a new car or a bigger house, or better clothes, these people knew, they were fully aware of the damage they were doing to the planet but they did not care. I walked to Zephyrus's side and gave him my arm and my thoughts as we left this level were "what next, how much more has man done?" " I wasn't the least bit ready to go on and see more but it was on to level 14 all the same."

125

CHAPTER SEVENTEEN LEVEL 14

Adultery

Zepherus:

"Kevin born January 10, 1975 in ft. Lauderdale father William mother Katie. Kevin is the youngest of three children. Dad owns a lawn care service they had a good life until his father left his mother for another woman when Kevin was seventeen years old. Kevin never forgave his dad for hurting his mom the way he did or for breaking up the family. His mom had taught him that God would always get them through any problems that arose and he would get them through this too. Although she dealt with the situation and kept her faith that all things happened for a reason life was never the same for them, but their life still went on Kevin went through school, fell in love married and they had two children. But this image of his dad never left him and instead of learning from his dads mistakes he began living the same way one girl after another lying to his wife. Kevin was trying to figure out what it was that his dad was looking for and how he could leave them and just start up a new family with someone else. Kevin's wife never thought not to trust him. She knew of the pain his father had caused in his life and never thought he would do the same to their children. His wife learned of his indiscretions when he was diagnosed with full blown aids and of course she had to be told. Fortunately for her she had not contracted this deadly disease but she could not live with Kevin any longer, she took the children and left Ft. Lauderdale and went back to her home town in North Carolina. Kevin died one night, alone in a hospital room there were no girls there to comfort him, and he no longer had a loving wife to sit by his side . Kevin played a deadly game and lost, this is where he will spend his eternity.

Adultery

Tamika born August 2, 1979 in Detroit, father Raymond mother Angela, she had one brother. Tamika married her high school sweetheart right after graduation. Jamar was the star quarter back on their high school foot ball team. His future and he was waiting for a football scholarship so that he could go to college. They had high hopes and dreams but when the offers never came she became disappointed in their relationship. He didn't work and he sat around being depressed and angry all of the time. They were on the verge of a breakup when word came that he had been accepted into one of the state colleges on a football scholarship. They were both happy but their problems were still hanging over their head. They couldn't let go of all of the angry words that had been spoken so he went off to school and she decide to stay behind until they had enough money put away so she would be able to join him. They talked quite often at first but then when she would call she wouldn't be able to reach him most of the time, and when she did reach him he was always too busy to talk anyway. Tamika grew lonely and started to go out with her friends on the weekends but most of them were still single and they would find guys to talk to and to dance with, Then one night she was sitting alone at the table waiting for her friends to finish their dance and this handsome young man asked her to dance and she figured why not. She was lonely and this guy had all the right words to say to her she left with him to talk over a cup of coffee and before she knew it she was in his apartment and in his bed. When this happened she realized that she didn't even care she didn't even feel the least bit bad. Her husband came home for the holidays and when he confronted her with the rumors that he had heard they had an argument and she left, called her boyfriend and he picked up at the coffee house down the street. They were driving on an icy road when they were broadsided by a truck Tamika died instantly of head trauma.

Zepherus:

"Sharon it is time for us to enter this level of deceit, Take my arm and be aware of all that you see."

Sharon:

"I did as Zepherus asked but I was afraid of what to expect next."

Zepherus:

"Sharon, man needs to be aware of his sins his hope lies in his remorse the only way to change his eternity is to ask for the lords forgiveness and change his ways. This look into eternity is to help man to change the way he is living so he does not have to end up on this level for an eternity, because once man has been graded and sent to a level there is no turning back he is there for eternity. Watch and remember what these adulterers will have to look forward to if they do not stop what they are doing and they pass over without remorse."

Sharon:

"Zepherus and I were standing outside of a club, I could hear the sound of music and laughter. As I watched from the window I could see men and women sitting at tables and at a bar they were talking a and some were holding hands and whispering in each other's ear they were laughing and having a good time, they looked as though they were so much in love I thought I was at a honeymoon resort but I noticed some of the people getting up from their tables and either going to the bar or going to sit at another table with someone else and the same thing was happening at that table and there right before my eyes these people started kissing and laughing, hugging, and holding hands and they were acting as if they were in love. The people at the bar were doing the same thing the moment they noticed someone getting up form a table they would rush over and take their seat. It was unbelievable, I watched as some of the couples got up and left together and when they returned they went looking for someone new to be with I saw arguments break out among some of the couples and every now and then name calling and fist fights began when someone moved in on what someone considered their territory but, the thing was that no one was anyone else's territory, no one belonged to anyone, what I saw was not love it was pure lust there was no caring it was absolutely nothing. This continued the whole time we were there they all went their own way, no love, no faithfulness, no commitment to any one, just a bunch of lonely sad pathetic losers with no one to love them and with no one to trust, happiness was not to be found anywhere on this level.

When I looked at Zepherus he had this look or total dismay on his face this was something I had not seen before. As I looked at the faces on these people I noticed they did not have the glow of the ones on the upper levels, they seemed drawn and haggard some of them looked as though they were sick and I brought this to Zephreuses attention."

Zepherus:

" Yes some of these people have passed over because of the aids virus, and some of them age quickly here they must see the pain of having to grow older and have someone younger take someone away from them. They live eternity with these physical changes happening to them It will never differ. There is no chance for happiness or true love for anyone here. The ones that were married and gave it all up when they decided to betray their partner and cheat or the ones that didn't care about breaking up some ones home or family because all they cared about was what they wanted ,a man or a woman to be with some because they were lonely, others because they wanted to be with some who had money or success, others wanted to be with someone with power, they wanted to shine off of someone else's success and it didn't matter to them who got hurt in the process, spouses, children it just doesn't matter to any of these human beings. I try not to judge these humans on any level but for some reason I cannot comprehend why someone would give away the love of a family for another human. I understand marriage can be difficult but what makes these humans not understand that difficult is a part of life. Your successes come from over-coming difficulties your strength comes from overcoming adversity. Life cannot always be the honeymoon or the perfection that is hidden in the unknown of a person, this is what man should accept before they engage in a lifelong relationship look and listen to everything, if you find there is something unacceptable in that person then do no continue the relationship. Sharon I hope that I have given you an understandable view of this level, I am a beta it is very difficult at times to express my view so that it is understood. Come take my arm so that we may leave this tragic level and go on to level 15"

Sharon:

"I walked to Zepherus and I took his hand and gave it a pat, I could see how much this level had disturbed him. "

Chapter Eighteen Level 15

Corruption

Zepherus:

"Mitch born April 8, 1979, in Pomona, mother Lacy father Mark, dad is a fisherman owns his own business mother is a homemaker. Mitch joined the police force right after he graduated from the community college. He always worked hard and had a lot of friends, no love interest to speak of He lived in a nice cottage on the beach liked nice things, expensive car, expensive clothes and lots of big boy toys, and being a police officer sometimes it was hard to get ahead but Mitch was always played it straight and was well respected by friends and co-workers. Then one night while partying in a cops bar he was approached by a fellow officer and asked if he'd like to make some extra money. Mitch had a few debts he wanted to clear up and asked what he'd have to do it was simple all he would have to do is go out on his dads boat with him and drop a package into the water that's it, there would be a homing device in the package and it would be picked up later by another boat. The only thing was he was not to ask any questions and he could tell no one and for this he would be paid one thousand dollars. Mitch didn't agree to do this at first but when he went home and thought about he knew he could use the money after all I'll only do it this one time. He called his friend and made the arrangements to pick up the package, he then called his dad and told him that we wanted to go out with him the next day it was all set. He picked up the package

131

went to the boat early and stashed the box in a place that would be easy to throw off the boat without being seen. The plan went off as expected he did exactly as he was told when they were out two miles in the water he pulled the tag on the package and dropped it over the side of the boat. It sank within seconds and no one was the wiser. When Mitch got back home and the package had been picked up he received his payment. Mitch thought "What an easy way to make a thousand dollars, I'll have to do this again." And he did time after time and the money kept rolling in. Then one day after picking the package up he noticed that it had a split on the side of the box. Mitch didn't bring the box aboard the boat that day in fear of the contents being damaged in the water so he tried getting hold of his friend to tell him of his decision but there was no answer. That evening when he got home he talked to his friend his friend warned him to keep the box safe and he would be there soon to pick it up. Mitch picked the box up and curiosity got the better of him, he twisted and turned the box until he finally got to peak into it, he thought he would find a package of marijuana but instead the package was filled with thousands and thousands of dollars. He looked the box over to see if there was a way to open the box without disturbing the homing device. Just then he heard a knock at the door, it was his friend to pick the box up. He gave him the box and was told that he would get a phone call when the package was ready to be picked up again. Mitch wasn't satisfied with the money he was getting for the risk that he was taking and wanted more after all he thought If I get caught there goes my job, my pension, my reputation and I could go to prison he could not complain to his friend because he might figure out that something was up and that Mitch knew what was in the packages that he was delivering and he couldn't take that chance. So Mitch figured out a way to open the package take some money out and reseal the box without the homing device being disturbed. He really thought that he was putting one over on these people he must have done this at least a half dozen times before his friend confronted him and told him that he would have to return all of the money he stole. When Mitch tried to deny the allegations his friend took his gun out of his holster and shot him in the head, Mitch died immediately from the gunshot wound."

Corruption

Zepherus:

"At this level we will encounter some of the people that have caused most of the moral destruction on the planet earth there is not a country in the world that is most affected by these people. They do not care about the lives they destroy every minute of every day. All these acts you are about to encounter are done for money, power or control. Three of the leading reasons all crimes are committed by mankind. This is the devils offerings to those involved in these crimes. His only thoughts are "I will give you what you want because now, I own your soul. I have taken you away from God and you are mine and you will do my bidding for me as long as I want you to. Then whenever I no longer have any use for you and I am ready I will take you and I will find another soul to own and to take away from God for eternity, there will always be the greedy and corrupt, my task is simple."

This level is their payment in eternity for being the cause of destroying so many lives. There is no way to stop these people on earth other than the destruction of mankind itself ,this is why you have been brought here Sharon to make it clear as to what eternity holds for them , they may just stop and think before getting involved in all this evil. Watch very carefully because the word must be brought back to earth with Gods warning. "Do on to others as you would want others to do onto you." Before we enter this level I will show you a glimpse as to where and how these crimes are committed."

Sharon:

"With those words word's we were standing in the middle of a city and we were shrouded in darkness I could hear the sound of music and laughter, Zepherus led the way and I followed him. WE were soon in the midst of night clubs, strip joints and sleazy hotels. There were hookers, pimps johns and drug dealers on every corner. I watched as the drug dealers made their deals right out in the open with people driving up in cars and stopping to make their deal, from hand to hand, money for drugs. The hookers were just the same as the drug dealers, the cars with the John in them would pull up the hooker jumped out counted their money and walked over to another car and then jumped in it, sometimes the hooker made her drug deal first before going over to the new John. She would show him her stash before getting in the car, they both smiled as though they were little kids eating candy. It was a vicious cycle girl after girl car after car.

Zepherus took my hand and led me through the door into the strip joint. I was amazed as he pointed out the number of prominent people that were there. Sitting at one table there was a judge and a counsel man, and the prosecuting attorney, sitting at the table across from them were some lawyers and police officials. They sat whooping and hollering as the girls danced and when they got up on their table they were putting one hundred dollar bills into the dancers, g- string. At another table sat a king pin in the drug trade with his entourage. I was amaze to see this drug king pin get up go over to the judges table and shake hands with the judge and everyone that sat at his table they were laughing, and making friendly comments and gestures toward each other. Pimps were making arrangements for their girls to take the men in the back room, it was unbelievable the john would hand the pimp the money and the wait at the hall entrance until the girl walked over him took him by his arm and led him to a room a little while later they came walking out as if they didn't even know each other.

Zepherus took me back outside and there we saw a couple of police go up to a hooker on the street and put her in the police car and drive away a few minutes they brought her back she didn't look very happy when she got out of the police car, the police just laughed and drove away.

We went on to another location this time we were in a warehouse and there were men selling stolen military weapons out of the back of trucks it's bad enough they are selling these weapons but these men were in the military and they were selling these stolen guns to the enemy who in return will use them to kill the innocent people of the war and the American soldiers but these people do not care who will be killed, the only thing they care about is who can pay the highest price. Our next stop on this journey takes us to an airport here private planes carry children from overseas to be sold into prostitution boys and girl alike as young s eight and no older than thirteen. These children are terrified their hands and feet are bound and their mouths are taped so no one would hear their crying, cattle are treated more humanly then these children. From the airport these children are taken to an old farm house where they are sold to the highest bidders from whorehouses, money, money it's all about the money. The next stop takes to a play ground where teens are selling drugs to other kids they didn't care about the damage they were doing to these other kids they liked what they were doing they liked being the big shot on the streets they being the one with the money. These drug dealers didn't stop to think that the people they get their drugs from are only using them to sell an illegal product for them and when you do get caught you will be the one going to jail because informing on your connection will mean death because these people do not fool around, this is a multibillion dollar business. Now that you're this big shot drug dealer you also have to worry about who wants you dead so that they can take over your territory. So I watched a these kids were in the playground selling their drugs when a gang of kids drove by and began shooting, end result two dead three wounded. Now there is a new drug dealer on the streets only this one is also a murderer."

Zepherus:

"Sharon what you have seen is only the tip of the ice berg. Sharon we do not have enough time to show you all of the corruption on earth but this some of the things the people have to contend with every minute of every day. Let it be known everyone of these crimes committed against man is witnessed and your judgment will be passé out the moment you pass over. Sharon it is now time to see how these people will spend their eternity."

Sharon:

"In a moment's time we were in a city again I recognized the strip joint we had visited earlier. Zepherus and I were once again inside. This time the people inside didn't appear as though people inside were having as much fun as they were having before the smell of stale alcohol cigarettes and cheap perfume filled the air and as I watched I could see that no one could get out they tried to get out the front door no luck they tried the back door, nope no luck there either, the windows uh, uh they couldn't even break the glass. These people that thought that they were having such a great time and didn't have a thought in mind as to what they were doing were now caught up in their little sleazy secret life for an eternity. All of the begging and pleading to let them out meant nothing to anyone.

As we left the club we again encountered the hookers and their Johns on the corner and I noticed that they would get into a car but the car could not go anywhere the furthest they could go was in and out of the car no matter how hard they tried they could not get the car to go anywhere, these people could not go home to their families, they could not go anywhere to eat other than a place that was close to where they did their business, they never seemed to change their clothes. The Johns and the police that took advantage of these girls and took their freebies rather than arrest them for what they doing also sat in their cars lock into this horror they would get out of their cars and try to walk away but they could go no further than the corner it was as if there was some sort of invisible wall because they could not step off of the curb or go around the block all they could do is turn around and walk back to their cars. They were trapped on these corners for eternity. I heard cries and whimpers but they fell on deaf ears. Their time to ask for forgiveness and change their ways was over and their past they could not change because there is no erasing what you have written in your book of life, and the choices we make are what we live with for eternity.

Our next encounter was at the farm house once again. I heard the sound of bidding I could feel the fear in the pit of my stomach as approached the entrance to the bidding room I did not know what I was going to see in there. After we entered the room and I watched for a while I saw, the sellers, the buyers and the auctioneers, but I was a bit confused about the merchandise they were bidding on. These were not children that I saw they were adults, and I watched closely. Once they were sold they were taken to the back room a little while later when they came back out they were shaking and trembling some had welts and bruises others had blood stains on their clothes they were stumbling and falling down as they now entered a cage that had a sign on it that read auctioneer. It was at that time I also noticed a sign on another cage that read bidder and the cage next to that that read sellers and the cage next to that read merchandise. It took a moment but it finally dawned on me as to what was going on here it was cycle, first you are the bidder then you are auctioneer then you are the seller then you are the merchandise. I almost had to laugh as I watched everyone as they took their turn on the bidding stand and waited to be taken in the back room knowing what was about to happen to them. Justifiably there was no mercy on these people just as they had no mercy on their victims. An eternity spent as your own victim.

The next sounds that I heard were that of rapid gun fire I watched as people were ducking and running I saw bodies on the ground and other people loading guns there were all types of people with different looks there were young and old alike, some were mercenaries some were gang bangers, some were terrorists, they all some kind of uniform to identify their cause or gang. Bang you're dead one minute, the next you're your back on your feet trying to duck, run or hide. The killing never ended there was no such thing as a cease fire. The longer I looked the more people I saw that were in the warehouse buying and selling weapons just like these. I turned and asked Zepherus if these people that are wounded or killed feel any pain."

Zepherus:

"They feel every bit of pain just like any human would feel, their crime on earth was to buy and sell these weapons and they were used to kill or harm and cause pain to another. Now they will spend their eternity trying to run from the pain and death that they have caused to other humans beings. "

Sharon:

"This next stop of this level brings us to a rally of sorts where there is a stage and a podium. On this stage men and women take their turn speaking only this is not like any rally I have ever seen. On the table next to the podium I see this gigantic book and I notice it has a list of names on in it and every one there is on this list they are all taking turns talking about whoever's name is on the list next and they all have the dirt to dish out about that person.

This is a tell all rally no one is left out from the incrimination every ones deepest darkest secrets are revealed payoffs, thefts, bribery, adultery, sexual predator, drugs involvement, child molestation, criminal activity, graft, abuse of power anything that someone thought they had gotten away with while on earth is shown and told in this room. If you have not asked for the lord's forgiveness and have not shown remorse, then your hidden secrets were never erased from this book and one at a time their name was entered onto the wall of shame to be seen by everyone for an eternity."

Zepherus:

"Sharon I am sure that you have seen enough of this level there is still so much more that you have not seen but I do believe you have seen enough to take home with you and I am sure that it will make quite an impact on those that commit these crimes.

Come take my arm as we go on to level 16."

Sharon:

"I once again wondered what next, what more, how much more evil is out there that mankind has allowed Satan to infest their mind with. I was about find out.

I took a hold of Zephyrus's arm and on to level 16."

CHAPTER NINETEEN LEVEL 16

Assault

Abuse

Zepherus:

"Norman, born February 10, 1960 in Newark his father is Arthur and his mother Ann he has four siblings two brothers and two sisters. Norman had to fight his way out of everything as a child he was the youngest of five children his dad was an alcoholic and abusive and his mother was always upset over one thing or another, house work, laundry the kids fighting the kids playing, cooking what the kids ate what the kids didn't eat. It was always drama and always abuse his mother thought nothing about hitting the kids in the mouth if they talked back the belt was his mothers number one form of punishment she didn't have to use her hands if she used the belt, but she could swing a punch too. His dad was just as bad when he came home from work drunk which was Monday thru Friday on the weekends he drank all day long. The kids were terrified to go to bed at night they never knew when he would come in their room and start beating them after listening to their mother's complaints. The children learned to cry quickly, otherwise he would not stop and you would get hit harder. This is how this child was raised and this is how he grew up to be a man.

Norman married and had two children and repeated what his father had taught him, violence, only he was also abusive to his wife. Joanna also came from an abusive family so she never thought that Norman could be like that after all he knew more than anyone what it was like to be abused they had already talked about this before they were married. Norman never drank alcohol when they first married and there was no abuse but as the children came along and his patients wore thin with the crying and noise that kid made so did the yelling and spankings. Joanne began to notice a pattern of her own abuse as a child and warned him to go get counseling for his problem and get it under control or she would take the children and leave. Norman promised that he would see a counselor but he never did, one morning when he woke up with a hangover he started yelling at the kids for making noise when he went to strike one of the kids Joanne stepped in to stop him he pushed her down and walked away he never even apologized for his actions he told her she had it coming for interfering when he was disciplining the children she told him if he ever raised his hands to her or the children again she would have him arrested. He promised it would never happen again and everything was good for a while then this one day when she was late getting home from work as soon as she walked through the door he began ranting and raving at her calling her vulgar names and accusing her of cheating on him he began to hit her and never stopped until she was unconscious on the floor the children were so frightened they ran next door and the neighbor called the police. Norman begged and cried and asked for Joanne's forgiveness but as much as Joanne loved him she loved living more, she knew that if she stayed with him he could kill her or even worse kill one of the children someday. Joanne divorced Norman, he remarried and Joanne never heard from him again. The last news Joanne read about Norman was that he had been arrested for the death of his new wife. Norman was convicted of her brutal death and died of lethal injection, Norman had no remorse for killing his wife he said she deserved it.

Abuse

Zephyrus:

"Sharon we have encountered many levels on our journey but the next few levels that we encounter are the most severe of them all these are the most depraved, corrupt, perverted acts against mankind here Satan rules these humans he has entered their mind and their soul there is no sense of judgment, no conscience, no remorse. These predators care about no one but themselves there is no such word as you in their vocabulary unless it is to accuse, "you did this to me, you made me do this to you, you are the cause of my anger." He only rights this person understands is his own right to do whatever he wants to do but his victims have no rights he will use control as a devise for mental abuse, he will use verbal abuse as a form of mental control and to keep you in control physically he will use physical force and financial control to keep you in need of him and to get what he wants anytime he wants or to cover up his indiscretions. Then he will cry and tell you how sorry he was and how much he loves you but this abuse will not just end the abuse does not stop it will become closer between beatings eventually someone may die either the wife from the beatings or the man from the defense or fear of the wife. Remember Sharon these people are incapable of love they only know of their own wants and needs like a possession their spouse or child or partner can be broken and thrown in the trash. Make these victims aware that he knows your fears for yourself and your family. No one knows any more then these victims what their spouse is truly capable of behind closed doors only they know of his threats and his anger. They are frightened and ashamed and they worry about how they will support their families if their husbands aren't there because he has all the money even though you work too he takes your pay check and pays the bills, and buys the food. They worry about what he will do if he thinks you are thinking about leaving him he has already taken away your car keys and threatened to lock you in your room, or he tells you if you do leave him he will find you and kill you because you are his and nobody else will ever have you and you wonder who will help me where do I go how do work because he knows where I work and he will follow me there or be waiting for me when I leave.

The black eyes the cracked ribs the punching and the kicking you in your stomach his hands around your neck squeezing the life out of you and only letting go moments before you pass out and running through your mind is the fear that you may die or when will I die at the hands of this man. Who is there to help, you're afraid to go to your parents he may hurt them and that is the first place he would look and if they knew what was going on he wouldn't let you go there anymore and a friends how could you involve them, call the police he would be back in an hour before you even had a chance to find somewhere to go and will he do as he threatens and kill you? Sharon this is what the abused must go through this is not an isolated incident it happens hundreds of times a day on the planet earth people are abused and killed by the one person that they should be able to trust their spouse after all if you can't trust your spouse who can you trust.

It is not always a spouse that goes through abuse sometimes it is a parent or a child. With a parent that has abusive children it is usually due to an inconstancy in family values. These children were not taught to respect their parents either one or both parent always gave in to these children every time they whined or cried or threw a temper tantrum. They worked hard to give the child everything and anything they wanted the only thing they didn't give them is discipline. When this child became demanding and selfish or threw a tantrum the parents would give in to him. If the child did not get what she wanted she hit her parents. Well, now this child is a teen and is screaming and cursing at her parents slamming doors and throwing things now this child is out of control and selfish the parents are at a loss and do not know how to deal with her. They cannot make her come home on time they cannot tell her what to wear who to hang around with they cannot even make her go to school if she decides she doesn't want to. Let's look down the road now this child is thirty and he cannot keep a job, she cannot stay in a relationship because no one is going to put up with a demanding selfish adult so even now when these adult children want or need something they still think the parents are responsible for the and they are still kicking and screaming when they don't get what they want.

The next part of this level upsets the balance in life itself although there are animals that may not have the instinct to nurture their young but they are rarely abusive to their young, man on the other hand will cause more pain and suffering to their young then any adult should have to endure. Innocent babies that should feel nothing but love and comfort from the ones who are responsible for their care yet these babies suffer from head trauma, shaken baby syndrome, broken limbs, starvation, dehydration, burns, bruises, abrasions neglect and abandonment. All of this before most of these babies can sit up or walk on their own. Can you imagine what it must be like to be attacked by a bear well think about what these babies must go through when they are beaten at the hands of their own parents, imagine how terrorized these little minds must be when they are thrown up against a wall or punched or kicked or suffocated, these helpless children of God. There are also the children that suffer at the hands of an alcohol or drug addicted parent, or the unwanted child or the child that is just in the way. There are children with birth defects that a parent doesn't want only because they don't want to have to care for them or the independent child that doesn't conform to every rule, the stubborn child that takes a little more effort to get through to, or the child that just can't sit still and the clumsy child that's always dropping or spilling things. What do you do with these kids do you look and shake your head and think that's kids for you or do you take a belt and beat them do you punch them over and over again until they lose their breath, do you kick them like they're a rag doll? Once they've fallen to the floor and are out of arms reach, maybe you beat them with a switch until you draw blood or maybe you lock them in a closet without food or water, when they refuse to eat something do you dump it over their head do you throw their plate on the floor and tell them to get down and eat it off of the floor like a dog and what about the back hands to the mouth do you ever stop to think about the damage you are doing to that child's mouth and all of the teeth you are destroying at the roots and when your child is twenty two and their teeth are dying at the roots this can be a great childhood memory. And to you the parent that has the audacity to call your child names or make fun of them these children are your product. To call your child stupid or lazy, fat, ugly useless, bitch, fagot, worthless if you tell them that you hate them or that you never wanted them or if you blame them for the failures in your life, what kind of a life are you setting them up to have? How can a child that has never known any type of love or kindness become someone capable of giving love or kindness or how can a child that has never experienced fun know what true fun is. If you take away a child's innocents and childhood because they live in fear of you or in fear of doing the wrong thing because it may make you angry with them who are you, what kind of a person could you possibly be? Do you come home from work and because you had a bad day look for something to complain about do you punish the kids because that's how you were raised?

Do you ever talk to these children? Do you ever stop to think that these little bodies are only children and look into their beautiful little faces? Can you ever see the humor in what they do or listen in amazement as they talk as they ask you about a butterfly or why the clouds move when they want to know why they can't see the wind? Can your child trust you enough to ask you about sex? Can your child tell you about the kid in school that's giving him a hard time? Can they come to you when their report card isn't all that great and trust you to say all the encouraging words they need to hear because I'm sure they have said all the other things to themselves already.

These Sharon are the acts that will cause these thoughtless uncaring people to enter this level for an eternity. The choice is theirs change their ways and show love and compassion to these children, have patience and a little bit of humor and their children will survive childhood and it may

143

help to keep them off of this level for an eternity. If you need help call on your father, ask God for his help in giving you the patience you need. Sometimes it is best to give that child to someone who will care and love your baby unconditionally, there is no shame in giving that child to someone who will love him, but there is shame in the abuse of that child. Ask and thou shall receive."

Sharon:

"The first thing I saw as we entered this level was a beautiful country setting. The sun was shining and the air was crisp and clear but in a moments time I jumped at the sight of a man attacking another man he was punching and kicking and hitting this man he was calling him all sorts of names but the other man did not fight back he never even tried to defend himself you could see that he was too frightened to do anything more than cower helplessly on the ground.

Zepherus and I walked a little further and we came upon a similar situation only this time it was two women and one was punching and kicking and hitting the other. I heard the woman yelling. "how many times have I told you not to touch my things? " the woman held a belt in one hand and the other woman's arm in her other hand so the woman could not get away, but like before this woman did not try to get away either she just cried out in pain from the thrashing she was getting.

We next approached another two men the one man had his hands around the other mans neck and was strangling him. The man could do nothing to help himself he could only lay there helplessly begging the man to let him go begging him to let him live.

As we walked once again we came across a woman sitting on a rock and she had a man over her knee and he had his pants pulled down and she was hitting him on his bare butt she hit him so many times she drew blood. He never moved he never tried to run away he just sat there crying and sobbing.

We again walked a little further down the road this time I could hear voices, as we walked over the ridge I could hear the sounds coming from this little make shift shed. "Please let me out I'm scared alone out here in the dark, there are spiders and bugs. I promise I will never do it again please. "But the man on the outside just laughed. "You'll get out when I'm good and ready to let you out and not a minute sooner you hear that boy." The man laughed louder and with that all you could hear were the cries the sobs and the whimpers as we walked away.

A little further down the road I once again heard this stern voice, "You are a useless piece of crap your lazy and no good you act just like a sissy you fat little fagot." When we got to where the voice was coming from there we saw two men, one was standing pointing his finger in the others face, the other man just stood there with his head held down he was so scared he wet his pants."

Zepherus:

"There is much more to be seen on this level Sharon but our time is running short and we must tale our leave. There is nothing more that can be said about this level these people can no longer be helped they are here for an eternity. I do pray that the message you bring back to earth will prevent this cruelty because once they have entered this level their justice will go on and on over and over never to end throughout eternity. Take my arm it is time for us to go on to level 17."

Sharon:

"I took a hold of Zephyrus's arm and I held tightly for some reason I just wanted to be sure that I wouldn't be lost somewhere."

CHAPTER TWENTY LEVEL 17

Molestation-Rape

Sharon:

"I don't know why but as I entered this level I felt much fear in my heart. I knew we were coming close to the end of our journey and many of the things I have seen so far have frightened me and I know every level we enter is worse than the one before I only pray that I can keep a clear mind so that I can remember all that I see on the levels I have yet to encounter."

Zepherus:

"Sharon I will need you to stay strong once we begin our journey through this level. It may become very graphic at times and you must pay close attention to the details. I have tried to protect you from most of the visuals on the other levels they pretty much describe themselves with having to see anymore than what you have already seen."

Sharon:

"We stepped out of the darkness into the vision of Grady."

Zepherus:

"Grady born March 20, 1972 in Phoenix, father Calvin mother Bonnie no siblings. Grady lived with his parents and his uncle he was a good student quite unassuming, he had few friends, liked riding his bike delivering news papers after school and swimming in his favorite pond. His uncle started to molest him when he was around twelve years old when his uncle took him on a fishing trip. It was a private spot where no one ever went and his uncle decided it would great to go swimming, his uncle jumped in the water naked this was a bit unusual Grady thought but he just brushed I off, he jumped in the water too while they were swimming his uncle talked him into taking his shorts off to. Then his uncle began touching Grady's butt at first Grady thought this was funny so he started doing the same to his uncle. Then his uncle grabbed him in the front Grady laughed because he thought his uncle had made a mistake but he did it again, Grady was embarrassed but tried laughing it off again before Grady knew it his uncle came up behind his and rubbed penis against Grady's behind. This time, Grady backed away from his uncle and turned and gave him a questioning look they swam some more but the uncle kept his distance from him after that they got dressed and headed for home Grady didn't even think about the incident again until the uncle came in to his room one night and climbed into bed with his Grady pretended to be asleep when his uncle grabbed his penis and started playing with it. Now Grady was a healthy young and curious boy and before he knew it he was enjoying the way it felt and when his uncle put his mouth on his penis he thought this feeling was great. When his uncle was done he just got up and left the room, Grady was ashamed and embarrassed at what he had let his uncle do to him but he was too embarrassed to tell any- one. This went on for months Grady was actually looking forward to his uncle's night time visit he never let his uncle know that he was awake but this one night when his uncle came into his room instead of putting his mouth on his penis he put his hand around Grady's mouth and turned him over and sodomized him Grady could not scream because he was so terrorized. Than his uncle whispered in his ear "If you tell anyone I'll tell them that you let me come in your night for months and that you liked what was going on." Grady didn't know what to do.

His mother noticed a change in Grady's behavior his school work was being affected he didn't hang around with any of his friends and he was avoiding his uncle she knew something was drastically wrong but when she approached him he ran out of the house in tears she talked to her husband and he said he would have a talk with his brother to see if he had any idea as to what was going on. When Grady's father approached the uncle and asked him if he knew why Grady was acting like he was toward him his brother became nervous and began to stutter that's when dad decided to have a talk with his son. When Grady's dad asked him what was wrong Grady broke down in tears and told his dad what his uncle had done. When his father heard this he ran outside to talk to his brother but his brother began to run and as he was looking back to see where his Grady's dad was he ran directly into a car on the road he died on impact. Grady went to counseling and eventually he came to terms with what had happened and he understood that his uncle was the adult making adult choices and that he was a vulnerable preteen with a curious nature."

Rape

Sharon:

"Zepherus next brought us to a place that was familiar to me I am a catholic so the church vestibule was a place where I had spent some time as a child but all my years in the catholic church did not prepare me for the sight of a priest with his pants down and one of the choir boys having oral sex with him. I wanted to die right there on the spot. When the boy was through and he got up he had a look of disgust and anger on his face. I heard him as he spoke to the priest. "Father I don't want to do this anymore." He said in a gentle tone.

"My son, my son, you know how much I love you. I could never have done something like this unless I believed you loved me too. You do love me, am I not correct?" The priest employed.

"Yes, I love you father." The boy told him in return.

"Then I will see you tomorrow. "The priest told him as he got up and escorted the boy to the door.

Zepherus walked up and took my arm and we left that place. The next place we entered was the bedroom of a little girl, she was sound asleep when her father came in to check on her he walked over to her bed bent down to kiss her goodnight but instead of leaving the room he climbed into bed with her he began to kiss her. she tried to push him away but she was so little he put his hand across her mouth so her whimpers could not be heard. He did not penetrate her but he opened her legs and rubbed himself on her crotch until he had a climax. He then told her she was daddy's little girl and to be sure that she doesn't tell anyone because mommy would be mad at her and she would send her away. He told her that this was her and daddy's secret that all daddies have secrets with their little girls. The little girl cried herself to sleep and did not tell any one of the pain she was going through, she feared her father's threats that her mom would send her away.

Zepherus once again took me away from there and brought me to a street where children were laughing and playing. I watched as this blue pickup truck stopped in the middle of the street to watch the kids. He watched a little boy as he was walking home from a baseball game he carried his bat and mitt on his shoulder. The man began to follow the boy until he was sure that he could not be seen. He pulled up next to the little boy and asked him if he had seen his little dog but the boy did not answer him he just kept walking the slowly followed him in his truck he asked to boy to look at the picture of his dog. The boy stopped to see and when he put his head in the window the man grabbed him hit him over the head and knocked him out. The only thing his mother found when she went looking for him was his bat and mitt. The next day the boy was found in a field a few miles away from his home he had been beaten and sodomized and left to die. The boy never fully recovered from his traumatic ordeal all because he tried to help a stranger look for his little dog.

Zepherus and I walked a little further this time we found ourselves at a shopping mall. There were people walking, laughing and talking as they shopped. I watched as a group of young girls were having something to eat at the food court.

Zepherus and I looked on as this man sat next to the girls and watched their every move. When the girls got up to leave he followed them, he watched their every move as they shopped, went to the bathroom and talked on the phone and he followed them as they left the mall. You could see that he was just waiting for the opportunity to do something. Then one of the girls went back Inside the mall to get change for the bus he followed her. After a minute or so he approached her and told her that one of her friends had asked him to tell her that they would meet her around the other side of the building because some of the boys were there. She thanked him and he left but he didn't go far he watched her as she went out the side door and he was right behind her. When she realized that no one was there she turned around to open the door but it had locked behind her. As went to walk around the building she ran right into the guy from the mall. She took one look at his face and she knew that she was in trouble. He grabbed her and covered her mouth with a cloth she began to get dizzy and he dragged her to his car. He sat her in the front seat and pretended to be talking to her as he drove off. One of her girlfriends spotted them as he drove by, she yelled to her and waved and when did not get a response she realized that her friend was in trouble. She quickly ran back inside the mall to find the other girls that had gone back in the mall to look for their missing friend. The girls called for security and security called the police. When the police got there the mall security gave them all the information they had available they had already gone through the security tape and they got the model of the car but because the kidnapped was aware of the cameras they could not get a license plate number or description of the man. He drove the girl to an abandon garage and raped and sodomized her I watched helplessly as he tore off her clothes forced her to have oral sex, raped and beat this young girl she screamed out in pain as he bit her but this man had no mercy . When he was through raping her he turned her over and sodomized her he left her lying on the filthy garage floor and before he left her walked over to her and ripped her necklace off of her neck. He went home took a shower placed the necklace in a box with jewelry that he had acquired the same way from other girls sat down ordered a pizza and turned the television on and watcher the reports of the kidnapping The police found the girl stumbling down the road clutching her torn clothes in her hands. She was bleeding and dirty and she could not stop sobbing. She spent two weeks in the hospital and when she got home she was terrified to leave her house. She knew that this man was still out there and maybe he would find her again.

Our next stop was in an apartment. There was a room set up with photographic equipment there were stuffed toys and satin pillows arranged on a mattress on the floor. Another section of the floor had a beach scene with a little umbrella, beach ball and sand built up around a small pool filled with water to simulate a beach. Within a few minutes two men came out of a bedroom with a little girl not much older than seven years old. She had on a tiny bathing suit and wore her hair up in a bun and she had on bright pink lipstick and eye makeup. I actually wanted to walk over there and pick this child up and take her out of there.

The man with the camera directed the little girl as to where she should sit the other man stood by and watched. The photographer was yelling orders at the child telling her how to pose, how to sit on the beach ball and then he told her to take off her bathing suit top, she did not want to do that. The man that had been watching walked over to the girl and grabbed her arms and shook her the little girl just stood there looking at the ground with tears flowing down her cheeks. The little Girl finally complied with the photographers request and took off her top he had her pose sitting on the beach ball with her legs open then he had her get into the pool and pose bending over, in the mean time he kept yelling at her to smile.

A few minutes later a little boy came out of the bedroom He was probably about a year or so older than the girl. He came out of the room with his head hanging you could tell this was not the first time these kids were in this position. The man that had been standing around watching the kids walked over to the boy and talked to him the boy shook his head in an agreeing manner and walked over to the girl. The photographer once again began to rattle off orders to both children. He had them pose holding hands, kissing and then he had them remove their bathing suits, all while he continued to take pictures. Both of these children were mortified. Next he had them pose on the mattress holding each other in one another's arms. It was one of the most disgusting things I had ever seen in my life and I couldn't help but wonder what kind of a pervert was going to buy these pictures, how could anyone get their enjoyment at such a cost to these little children. After another hour went by and the perverted photographer was finished he let the kids get dressed. When the kids went into the bedroom, the photographer paid the other man walked over and closed up his equipment and left. When the kids returned to the room the other man took them with him. As they were leaving I heard him tell the kid's "if you want to eat you'll do what you have to do. If that lazy bitch of a mother didn't leave you she'd be doing this instead of you." I heard the boy as he turned and looked at the man and said "o.k. dad."

I could not wait to leave this place I could not stomach any more of this perversion. I remember thinking to myself "I will never think of men in the same way again seeing all of this has probably changed my life forever, how would know who to trust in your life, how will these children ever survive after the things they have had to go through? I had to wonder too about the parents of these children I had seen on this level, how will the parents ever survive the trauma of seeing their child hurt? The pain and anguish they feel will live in their hearts forever.

The next stop on this journey brought us to a woman in her bedroom. She lived on the second floor of an apartment building her bedroom window had a fire escape with a ladder, her window was open a crack we watched as this man entered her room. He wore a face mask and rubber gloves. He crept to her bed and when he got close enough he covered her mouth and put a knife to her throat, and he told her if she said one word made just one whimper he would kill her. He taped her mouth and wrists with duct tape cut off her pajamas with the knife, he raped her and before he left he told her he knew where she lived and where worked and where she goes at night and if she goes to the police he would find her in one of these locations and the next time he saw her it wouldn't be sex she would have to worry about. He got up left her hands and mouth taped and went out the window as quietly as he had entered.

Rape

Our next encounter was at a university we stood at a bridge walkway.

It was dark and we saw this young woman as crossed the bridge she was so engrossed in fumbling with her school books she never saw the man coming from under the bridge he grabbed her and before she knew what was happening she was on the ground being dragged underneath the bridge she was being punched an hit then she felt something tight being pulled around her neck she was being strangled she felt light headed and fainted. When she woke up she knew that she had been raped her clothes had been torn off and thrown to the ground and she was doubled over in pain. "Who can I tell I never even seen the person who did this to me? " She sat on the grass as she tried to put her clothes back on and cried."

Zepherus:

"Come Sharon take my arm we have seen some of the horrors that these humans have had to endure at the hand of man now we will see where and how they will spend their eternity."

I know how these children's suffering has affected you and I know that their suffering is an injustice to them the innocent victims of Satan's power on earth. This we cannot change but God is here to pass out judgment on these evils that have depraved indifference to mankind.

Here in heaven there is no Satan there is no one here to protect his soldiers. There is only justice for those that were unjust, to those whose minds were so devoured by the power of Satan that they could not feel any remorse for what they did to any of their victims. Their minds are an empty shell to feelings or emotions they care about nothing but their own needs. They are as an animal would be that is on the prowl these evil deeds are what sustain them. They do not see the beauty in a child's smile or the innocence of laughter they do not see the joy in their play. They only see them as prey, as food to feed their hungry perversions"

Sharon:

"Zepherus this is truly terrifying to me. How are we to protect our children, how do we keep them safe?"

Zepherus:

"I have no answers for earthly things I can only ask that those on earth listen closely to their guides to be more aware of their presence and to what they are trying to tell you. Do not double guess your fears they may just be your guide trying to get your attention to protect you from harm. It may just save your life someday."

Sharon:

"Then may I ask you, what is the reason for prayer? People pray for the protection of their loved ones to keep them safe and every day our children suffer and die from disease, accidents and murder. Women and children are raped at the hands of these depraved individuals. Many of them die."

Zepherus:

"Sharon, God has always answered your prayers he hears and sees all. Prayers are your worship they are your alone time with God. This when you ask your will but this is not all one sided you must trust in his word to you. Remember, your time on earth is known to the lord the day you are born life is a schedule you are on death is an appointment you must keep. Death comes when you have completed what God wants you to do. This cannot be changed and the children, they are on loan to you, you do not own them, they are Gods children they are entrusted into your hands until it is time for them to come home again. It is your suffering that you must endure. The child lost is at home with their father never to suffer any pain or heartache again. You have prayer, yes and God has listened although he would not stop the moment of death he was there for your child and he protected them from any pain they would have endured. Your guardian is there to protect you from all physical pain. The child was only aware of the thought of their loved ones before they crossed over. Now your faith is what God offers you so that you may survive on earth until your day of reckoning is here. Here is where your loved one awaits you.

Do not let Satan come into your heart at this time, remember he exists in the dark and will try to enter your mind and blame God for your loss. He will be there trying to take control, in this moment of sorrow and weakness."

Sharon:

"Thank you Zepherus you have taught me well." "Zepherus held out his arm to me so we could leave this place and go on to the end of this level.

We were on the edge of a river when I heard someone running through the woods. I looked from where the noise was coming from and I saw two men one was of medium build with brown hair and a straggly beard. The younger man was thin with light brown hair and he was clean shaven. The older man caught up with the younger man and threw him down on the ground and was pulling his clothes off and he was punching him in the head, once he got his clothes off he turned him over and sodomized him the older man turned the younger man over again and punched him in his face breaking his nose. The younger man tried to defend himself but he had no strength to fight him off. When the older man was through raping and beating the younger man he got up pulled his pants up a kicked the man on the ground and walked away. The younger man lay there on the ground holding on to his pants and cried.

We walked a little further and came to a an old house in need of repairs as we entered the house we could hear the sound of cries coming from the bedroom we walked into the bedroom and watched as a man was being molested in the bed. His legs and arms were tied with tape and he was being forced to have oral sex by another man. When the finished he got up and just left the other man lying on the bed with his hands and feet bound.

The next thing we encountered was on a city street it was dark and the street was quiet. A man stood on the corner waiting at a bus stop when he was approached from behind grabbed around his neck and dragged behind a building. He was punched and threatened with a knife his pants were torn off and he was raped and left lying on the ground beaten and bloody he didn't even have the strength to get up and call for help so there he lay on the ground, crying and whimpering a few minutes later we found ourselves on a dark country road. There pulled over to the side of the rod was a man with a tire jack in his hand trying to figure out how to change his tire when a man pulled up in another car and offered to help him. The man walked over to the car smiled, talked for a minute and picked up the ties wrench lying on the ground next to the man trying to fix his tire. As he bent down to change the tire he swung around and hit the other guy with the wrench knocking him un- conscious. He stood up and dragged the man into his car and drove away he pulled off the road raped the man and cut his throat threw him out of his car and left him for dead as he drove away. I turned to Zepherus In utter shock, and said to him ,"There is so much violence at these levels Zepherus, but it seems as though only one person is being retaliated against." He looked at me for a moment his head bent in thought."

Zepherus:

"Sharon you are only seeing one side of the coin as you on earth say. These are never ending battles this time you are the perpetrator the next time you are the victim and it goes around and around from one act to another. Always remember what ye have sown ye shall reap.

Sharon Take my arm I believe you have seen enough of this perverseness. It is time for us to go on to level 18."

Sharon:

"I was thankful to Zephyrus for taking me out of this level but I also feared where we would be going next."

CHAPTER TWENTY-ONE LEVEL 18

Murder

Zepherus:

"Casey born December 17, 1979 in Wichita, father Allen mother Jean. Casey was the oldest of three children. He was always an honor roll student in school. But from an early age Casey stayed to himself, he never wanted to be bothered with other children this included his siblings, he never abused them he just stayed away from them he would go outside or to his room when anyone was around. His mom and dad tried to get him to interact with other children but he didn't like sports and he didn't like the boy scouts, there wasn't much other than his school work and reading magazines that interested him. He liked science and dissecting small animals. He said he always wanted to be a surgeon. Casey graduated at the top of his class in high school and went on to a prestigious collage. He never dated in high school and it appeared that it would be the same in collage because he was in his third year and still never found anyone he cared enough about to go out with more than once. Casey was a good looking boy but his unfriendliness kept people away from him and further more he didn't care one bit, he actually liked it that way.

One night after leaving the library he bumped in to a girl from one of his classed they talked for a few minutes and went their separate ways then they ran into each other again at school they really seemed to enjoy others company . He asked her out she said yes and that was it they started dating but Casey couldn't seem to get as involved with her as she wanted him to and he began to get annoyed after she accused him of seeing other girls, he barley had enough time for her and his school studies let alone another girl and he wasn't about to let this inter fear with his life so he told her that he didn't want to see her anymore at least not until the end of the semester. She seemed a little upset but told him that she was o.k. with that.

Soon after that all kind of things began to happen to him. He came out of school to go to work and he found out that he had two flat tires on his car. He looked around and scratched his head, one tire he could fix himself but two now he would have to call a service station and have a tow truck pick up his car after all he only had one spare. Casey didn't think anymore about the tires until a few days later when he went to unlock the doors and couldn't put the key in the lock it had been glued. That's when Casey realized someone was messing around with him but he could not figure out who would do something like that to him. He called the campus security and reported the incidents but they told him there wasn't much to do without an eye witness. He called off of work and had to call a service man to come unglue the doors. The following day he went class and when he returned to his apartment his room had been trashed, his clothes were cut with a knife his papers had been destroyed and his sheets had ketchup poured all over them. Once again he called security all they could say was that he must have made someone really mad at him. That afternoon he ran into the girl he broke up with. He was really glad to see her after all she was the only friend he had. They went out to get something to eat and she started questioning him again and Casey knew something wasn't right and then it dawned on him that he didn't have any one else that would be angry with him, who else would have done all these things to him he stopped her cold he knew right then and there that no one else could have a reason for doing these things to him but when he confronted her she started yelling at him that it has to be one of his other girlfriends doing this to him. He told her to stay away from him and his things otherwise she would end up in jail. The girl turned around and slapped him in the face then turned and ran out the door before he could stop her. Casey went directly to the campus security and this time they had a talk with her, notified the campus administrator and she was called in for a conference it seems she had a similar incident at her previous collage and had been suspended from that school because of it. Due to the allegations made at the other school she was suspended until a formal hearing was arranged. She was furious with Casey She left school and Casey didn't hear from her again. A few months later Casey received a get well card in the mail he laughed about it for a minute then he realized who it was that most likely sent the card to him which made him feel quite uneasy as he walked outside cautiously looking around to see if she was anywhere around then he laughed to himself, shook his head and began to cross the street to where his car was parked. Casey got about half way across the street when a car came speeding towards him it was impossible to get out of the way he was struck flew fifty feet into the air before he landed in the middle of the street ,he died in the ambulance on his way to the hospital. The girl crashed into a pole and died on impact. "

Zephyrus:

"Sharon, take my arm as we enter this next level with some of Satan's most evil followers."

Sharon:

"I was terrified at where we were about go, I could feel my hands shake as I reached for Zephyrus's arm.

Murder

Sharon:

"As we enter this level we are in the darkness of a city in decay there are no street lights the only light comes from the glow of fire burning in trash cans there is graffiti on everything in sight and garbage is laying all over the street, Styrofoam containers, newspapers, bottles, cans and bags. There was barley a palace to walk where you weren't stepping over garbage. The smell from the sewers was over powering. There are cars in the street with their tires flat and dry rotted they are covered in rust and dirt it looks like a city after a nuclear attack. I caught a glimpse of a man out of the corner of my eye as he ran across the street into a doorway he was dressed in dark clothing with the hood of his sweatshirt pulled up around his head I could not see his face in the dark shadows. I heard the footsteps of someone running up the sidewalk he ran directly to the man hidden in the doorway. I watched as he raised his arm and I caught the reflection of a knife as his arm came down he began stabbing the other man over and over again until he fell to the ground in a pool of his own blood arms wrapped around his stomach as if he was trying to relieve his pain. He laid on the ground his body motionless as though he was dead. The man with the knife watched for a moment and fled into the darkness.

When I looked back to see the man in the doorway he was struggling to get to his feet. He stood up still holding on to his stomach and ran away.

I looked at Zepherus and I told him I knew this man was dead yet he got back up on his feet and ran away."

Zepherus:

"Remember what I have told you, this is their eternity, on earth as it is in heaven. This was their choice to live an eternity in fear, pain, suffering and death and to relive that fear, pain, suffering and death over and over throughout eternity."

Sharon:

"Zepherus and I spoke as we walked and we soon came to a house on a neighborhood street. The yard was overrun with weeds and an old bicycle lay rusted and twisted in the driveway with weeds entwined in the spokes. I could hear sounds outside the house and I smelled the fumes of gasoline I could see the shadow of a man as he poured gasoline around the perimeter of the house lit a match and set the house on fire. I looked on as the house burned and I heard the screams from a woman coming from inside the house as the man fled I could hear the faint sound of laughter. In a matter of minutes a woman in flames came running out of the house she screamed as she threw herself on the ground and began to roll around to put the flames out. Her body was burned to a crisp her hair singed to her head and her clothes had melted to her body. The woman sat there elbows on knees her head in her hands as she cried out in pain. The woman then got up and ran into the night. We walked a little further and we were in a shed, a man was strangling another man with a rope when the man appeared to be dead he put him on a table and cut off his head and after talking to the head for a minute he threw it in a bag. Then he cut off his arms and put them in another bag he then sawed the man in half removed the legs and put those body parts in another bag, we watched as the man dragged the bags into the woods and scattered the body parts. I remember thinking well this is really over for this guy but no sooner had the thought passed through my mind right there in front of my eyes the body parts began to move and roll around until they all pulled together and he became whole again he stood up and struggle to walk away moaning and groaning the whole time.

My head was throbbing from watching all this horror when the sound of gun fire brought my attention back to my surroundings. The sound of the gun shots rang in my ears. I saw two men running down a dark ally. When the men reached the end of the ally the man with the gun pointed it at the other man first he shot him in the arm then the knee then the other arm and then the other knee as the man crumpled to the ground the man with the gun waited for a minute with the gun pointed at the man's head he laughed and pulled the trigger putting a bullet right between the guys eyes killing him instantly. But once again the man that lay dead on the ground got up leaned against the building for a moment and stumbled away. I never saw two people together where one wasn't killing the other. Night never turned to day it remained pitch dark at all times. I thought it was time to leave this level when I heard the sound of fighting Zepherus and I walked around the corner and there we came upon all of these people brawling, men as well as women. They had pipes and chains, knives and fists all going at the same time. One by one they fell dead to the ground until only one was left standing and he limped away. Then after a few minutes they started to get up one at a time and they walked or ran away all going in different directions. I remember thinking at that moment that I would rather be dead then have to live like this then the realization set in, they are dead and this is how these people will spend their eternity."

Zepherus:

"I know that you had a difficult time at this level Sharon but our journey is coming to an end we have but two more levels to view and we need no introduction at these levels, they will speak for themselves. Take my arm and we go on to Level 19."

Sharon:

"I did as Zepherus asked and gladly took his arm, I had mixed feelings though, I was anxious to go on because I knew our journey was about to end but I was hesitant because I didn't know what to expect. What more was there left for me to see?"

CHAPTER TWENTY-TWO LEVEL 19

War Mongers

Sharon:

"When we entered this level I could hear the sound of gunfire and bombs in the background. The sky was gray and we were on a rocky hill facing the desserts sands. As I looked around I could see many men all dressed in different uniforms. There was not a nation on earth that was not represented and they were her in the thousands upon thousands. All dying at the hands of other soldiers they fell to their death only to return to battle to die again there is nowhere to run there is nowhere to hide no way to escape their reality of what is going on around them. Time after time they relive the pain of death the agony of their wounds. I turned to Zepherus and asked why all of these soldiers were here, soldiers fight to protect their country."

Zepherus:

"War is killing and these soldiers have been paid to kill. They have no sense of justice they are only here to reap the benefits from someone else's suffering. To send your people into war for some abstract ideal you have of the way you want things to be, this is an injustice. To invade another country because you think they should live your way this is an injustice. To fight for riches or oil or to use the earth's natural resources as ransom against the world this is an injustice to all of mankind find a way to change your resources now while you still have the chance because those in control of the economy will control the earth.

Sharon, speak to those on earth about the meaning of justice and how it should be served. To protect those that are persecuted and under control, to protect those that live with tyranny and oppression to protect those against the threat of genocide because of race or religion. This is justice, to protect your country from the hands of such evil. But to kill and maim to keep you people under control this is unforgivable. To teach your people to kill without trying peace efforts is not in the best interests of those that you are responsible for. Are you in this for your own glory to be worshiped or held in the highest esteem by the people you have sworn to protect? War is not a game to be played with the lives of other humans. Everyone has the right to live a full life it is easy to put someone else's life on the line to die, but are you willing to do the same of yourself or your family members or do you hide in the safety of your homes or shelters while others die for you and your family. What is it that you offer these people in exchange for their life and what prayers do you offer to God at night? Come we have seen enough of this level, do not forget what you have heard or seen here this is a very important message to bring back to mankind. Take my arm to level 20 and the final level of our journey."

Sharon:

"I took a hold of Zephyrus's arm once again as we went on to the final step of our journey."

CHAPTER TWENTY-THREE
LEVEL 20

Atheists

Sharon:

"As we entered this level there was nothing but darkness I could not see my own hand as it held on to Zepherus. I was terrified I could hear movement but I did not know where it was coming from I did not know who or what was out there with us. I told Zepherus how afraid I was because I couldn't see anything, there was nowhere to go we couldn't walk because I wasn't sure whether I would fall into a hole or who I might bump into, if there was someone there. "Zepherus what kind of a level is this or did I open my eyes too soon between Levels?" He held tightly on to my arm and spoke gently to me."

Zepherus:

"No Sharon you did not make a mistake you have not been caught between levels. This is our last level on our journey and what you see is how these people will spend their eternity in total darkness, in nothingness, this is how they believed their eternity would be. They believed in nothing more after death. There is no other level for them to go to. They cannot go forward and there is nowhere they can go back to. It is now time to leave this level. Keep a tight hold of my arm and I shall take you back to where our journey began. "

"Sharon:

"I did not let go of Zephyrus's arm for a moment I held on tightly, I was so happy to know that this was the last step we had to take through the levels and I was not about to be lost now."

CHAPTER-TWENTY FOUR

The Final Good-By

Sharon:

"When I let go of Zephyrus's arm we were back where we were before we began our journey through the levels we were back at the doorway to Mary's office."

Zepherus:

"It is time my friend to say our final good-bys. Our journey has been long and you have seem much that you must bring back to earth with you I know we will be forever in each other's thoughts and your journey home will bring you many trials and many sorrows but remember our time together and the journey you have traveled here, may it bring you hope when you feel despair and strength when you feel weakness, courage when feeling abandon and alone. Remember the peace and the joy and the love our Father has given us not only as betas but for all of mankind as well. Be alert and listen clearly to your guide and follow your wisdom do not let man deter you from the path you must travel. Most of all have faith in what has been given to you. We will be watching over you at all times. We will meet with Mary one more time before you take your leave of us here and return home."

Sharon:

"Zepherus and I once again went through the doors to Mary's office she was sitting at her desk when we entered and stood to greet us. "

Mary:

"Sharon and Zepherus it is so wonderful to see you upon your return, we have been monitoring your journey at conference. I know how difficult this has been for you Sharon we chose Zepherus to take you on this journey because we believe he was the one to make you feel the safest and his knowledge of earth's ways is what would help guide you. Thank you Zepherus you have done your job well and showed the messenger everything she needed to observe. There are a few more words I have for you to take home with you Sharon. There are people on earth that suffer from many physical and mental inflictions, they have lived with disabilities most of their life and the pain and suffering that they have to endure is incomprehensible, it is not the physical struggle alone that these people have had to endure but the mental anguish as well they must live with the ignorance of those that do not understand or those that are fearful of their disability and have reacted in a cruel and disrespectful manner toward them. Tell them that it is their faith and trust in God that will give them their rewards in heaven and when they enter our kingdom they will be free of all the suffering they had to endure on earth. This Sharon Is my final message to bring back to earth with you, have tolerance of that which you do not understand show love in your everyday living be kind in spirit and gentle in words when you see someone struggling offer them your hand, when you see a person with a disability think of the daily struggle they must endure just to be able to tie a shoe or dress themselves or eat with a fork some have difficulty walking yet they do not complain nor do they look for your sympathy they endure and accept who they are and how they must live and ask only for respect in return. Take the time to say hello you may be amazed at their wisdom because it is beyond what most people could comprehend. Remember my words to you and we here in heaven will await you. It is the hour for you to now take your leave of us you must enter these doors to take your journey home. I give you my blessing and bid my farewell."

Sharon:

"With that Mary kissed my cheek and left the room. "Thank you Zephyrus, I only hope that I can remember all of what I have seen and to be able to express it so that it makes sense to those that listen. I promise you though I will always know the love I felt and I will never forget the strength and wisdom of the betas". "I reached over and gave Zepherus a kiss and squeezed his arm one last time. I turned and walked through the doors to the angel waiting inside for me."

CHAPTER TWENTY-FIVE

The Awakening

Sharon:

"My mind was in a haze as I woke to the sound of beeps and pumps pounding in my head.

I tried to focus as I scanned the room.

What am I doing here in a hospital?

As my head began to clear and I began to remember......

"Oh my God....!!! Oh my God !!!"

ACKNOWLEDGMENTS

"I cannot do this alone!! I cannot do this alone!!" Once I truly realized that what I kept telling myself over and over again was truth, only then was I able to let other people into my private world of dreams and visions. They kept me afloat with their faith support and commitment. Words cannot express the gratitude I hold in my heart for each and every one of you.

To Jennifer Baldwin my sounding board, my best critic my friend my daughter my strength.

To Sharon Irizarry My lifelong friend and right arm, without her faith I would have given up long ago.

To Jamie Grange and Chrissy Hussar, who spent hours on typing and printing copies of the manuscript so it could be shared with so many others, without your unselfish caring and help I would still be staring at a pile of notes and pages on my dining room table not knowing how to put it all together.

To Joni Canastrano your blind faith, extraordinary talent and imagination brought life to the cover of the C.D.

To Pat Mc Carthy, Liane Naples, Jennifer Bladwin and Sharon Irizarry, our weekly meetings kept the visions fresh and the purpose alive.

To Kenny Baldwin my son-in-law, biggest fan and cohort I love you. Your amazing talent for putting the C.D. together surpassed my dreams.

To Tony Pacella, who sat through meeting after meeting with us women, while he gathered information for a video he wants to produce for our web site, I don't know how you kept coming back to all of us week after week but you did and we all thank you. You are amazing.

To Lori Hassett, Helene Mason, Rose Witaszek, Debbie Sullivan, Deb Barr (Paper Book Trading Co.) Dog ears book Store, and many, many more of you who shared with us your reviews and opinions you gave me the confidence to say to myself" o.k. I'm ready, I can do this."

To The Messingre Woods Wildlife Care and Education Center, Inc. Who's hospital, rescue and release program is dedicated to preserving the health and life of our wildlife community and returning them to their natural habitat, .you are Earths Angels, a dedicated winged mass of loving caring staff, volunteers, Veterinarians, members and supporters that dedicate their time to this non- profit organization so that even the smallest of Gods' creatures have a chance for quality in their lives. I thank you for being such an influence on so many people. Everything that I have seen in this organization is about caring, respect understanding and commitment to others, let it be the birds and animals they deal with and tenderly care for or the people they so lovingly depend on to help make this organization a success. The world could learn much if they only followed your beliefs in humanity.

I truly believe God has placed you all in my life for a reason as you all helped me to reach the final steps of my journey.

I also want to thank the people who read the manuscript and disagreed with what they read. I too am committed to the fact that God is an all loving God and I respect your beliefs but I can only stand by what I saw and I cannot change any part of that.

To my husband Dan, who had to listen to me every day, he shared my fears, my sorrows and my laughter but on May 15 2007 God called him home .I am so sorry that you never got to see the end results. You would have loved to finally hear me say, "ex post facto,(It's all done.)"

"I love you all.

Sharon L. Burke